# THE REDEMPTION OF AN

# AFRICAN WARLORD

# THE REDEMPTION OF AN AFRICAN WARLORD

## THE JOSHUA BLAHYI STORY:

### A MODERN DAY CONVERSION FROM SAUL TO PAUL

## JOSHUA BLAHYI

A.K.A. GENERAL BUTT NAKED

DESTINY IMAGE₈ PUBLISHERS, INC.

P.O. Box 310, Shippensburg, PA 17257-0310

*"Promoting Inspired Lives."*

This book and all other Destiny Image, Revival Press, MercyPlace, Fresh Bread, Destiny Image Fiction, and Treasure House books are available at Christian bookstores and distributors worldwide.

For a U.S. bookstore nearest you, call 1-800-722-6774.

For more information on foreign distributors, call 717-532-3040.

Reach us on the Internet: www.destinyimage.com.

ISBN 13 TP: 978-0-7684-4207-6
ISBN 13 Ebook: 978-0-7684-8740-4

For Worldwide Distribution, Printed in the U.S.A.

1 2 3 4 5 6 7 8 / 17 16 15 14 13

# DEDICATION

I dedicate this book to the people victimized in my days of ignorance when I was blindly running the devil's evil errands. I dedicate it to all those who died, and all the children who became orphans. I dedicate this book to my kinsmen who died in their ignorant service to Nya-ghe-a-weh.

I also dedicate this book to my spiritual children worldwide, especially to Mundemba and Cameroun.

With open hands, I dedicate this book to whomever will read it.

# ACKNOWLEDGMENTS

I wish to thank and acknowledge God Almighty for giving Christ Jesus, His beloved Son, for a sinner like me.

I thank my mother. It is almost unbelievable she could show affection to me as a mother after knowing the much dreaded General Butt Naked was her own son.

The Lord has transformed me through another wonderful woman who I cannot leave out in this time of my life, Dr. Lyn Westman. God brought her into my life by way of her counseling skills, and she has shown me love that I cannot imagine. She even adopted me as her son.

I acknowledge and appreciate Bishop John Kun Kun of Liberia and Pastor Jare Olawaye of Nigeria who serve as my spiritual fathers and did not listen to threats and other disapproving comments. And I will not forget Soul Winning Evangelical Ministries.

Acknowledging due regard to my beloved wife, Josie, for accepting the brutal material that I was—yet she gave me every opportunity to prove myself and supports me while I fulfill the purpose of God for my life through this book and other areas.

To Reverend David Nehemiah Greene who risked his life to aid me in escaping Liberia, in obedience to the Lord. He stood by me throughout my life in exile and since I returned to Liberia.

To Musu Kawah who first recognized the greatness God put in me. She made efforts to set the stage for me to effectively utilize my potential.

To Mrs. Jean Seah Jabbal who opened her home to me when other homes were afraid of me; she even introduced me to the Church of God in Christ.

My special acknowledgment to the Church of God in Christ family and the Community Of Caring (COC) family through Mother and Elder Charles C. Kennedy. To the Late Mother Hazz, may she rest with the Lord.

My great acknowledgment to Harris T. Warner who strived to reconcile me with the people on whom I inflicted pain, and for the time he gave in the arrangement of these testimonies.

My acknowledgment to Evangelist Ceebee C.D. Barshell who interpreted these deep truths into an understandable language.

Finally, to all the families the Lord has given me around the globe, especially in Nigeria, Cameroon, Ghana, Benin Republic, Togo, Cote D'Ivoire, and Singapore.

# ENDORSEMENT

Joshua Milton Blahyi is a young, dynamic man called by God from his mother's womb. I strongly believe that God only allowed him to go on reconnaissance for those fourteen years he spent in the kingdom of darkness. This book is written to expose the deeds of the kingdom of darkness and to reveal the awesome power and tangibility of God's love to humankind.

Evangelist Blahyi and his testimony in this book are tools and weapons of liberation for the Body of Christ to use. If the Body of Christ reads and responds to the deep revelation of this book, it will bring the end of the devil's deception in our lives, marriages, businesses, and ministries. In the years to come, the Church is going to experience serious attacks from the devil. The ignorant and the fainthearted won't stand a chance. Read this book, increase your knowledge, and launch an advanced and aggressive spiritual warfare. Read it prayerfully, carefully, and with an open heart.

EVANGELIST JOHN KUN KUN
Soul Winning Evangelistic Ministries, Inc.
Barnesville Estate Monrovia
Liberia, West Africa

# AUTHOR'S SPECIAL CHARGE

This book would not be complete if I don't share this burden the Lord dropped into my spirit. I want to admonish Christians worldwide to stand in the gap to intercede for God to touch the hearts of international and national policy makers to revisit their imprisonment laws. I have learned firsthand that many prison inmates come to their senses just a few minutes before they are thrown into jail.

Children of God, the world is waiting for the manifestation of the sons and daughters of God, so we need to stand our ground in prayer. If you are in the position to reach out to prisoners, please help to free them from their self-imprisonment by sharing a copy of this book with them. Tell them that although they are jailed by chains and bars, telling the truth of their stories could help others, and by this they will enjoy a sense of freedom in Christ Jesus.

Those who are related to convicts, please do your best to stand in the gap for your relative. Who knows? God might want you to be used as a hero, like all the people I acknowledged in this book and in my life. After reading this book, you will understand that your relative's offense cannot be compared to mine. You will soon realize how terrible I was; but, like the apostle Paul, the same person the worst came from is the very person through whom God is now working. I also agree that many might not seem to comply to reasoning, but it is not for us to give up on them.

Proverbs 4:16 states that the wicked do not sleep until they do evil. Let us keep standing until God—who is faithful and responsible for all of us—decides their end.

*To open their eyes, in order to turn them from darkness to light, and from the power of Satan unto God, that they may receive forgiveness of sins and an inheritance among those who are sanctified by faith in Me* (Acts 26:18).

# CONTENTS

# FOREWORD

Not since the conversion of Saul of Tarsus on the Road to Damascus have I ever heard a conversion story more radically compelling than that of the former African warlord, General Butt Naked. To those who are discouraged thinking that you have "unreachable" friends or loved ones, this story will encourage and convince you that there is no one beyond God's loving grasp. To those are struggling with overcoming the shame of their own past, as many Christians are, this book will inspire you to receive Christ's total forgiveness for yourself. To those who are wondering if God still works miracles today, Joshua's supernatural testimony will provoke you to believe, beyond any doubt, that God is the same yesterday, today, and forever.

Having ministered alongside Joshua Blahyi in both mass crusades and the most notorious ghettos in Liberia, I am still in awe of the grace of God in this man's life. He is one of the most gentle, kindest, and most Christ-like people I have ever been privileged to meet. There were many moments while ministering with Joshua that I would look at him in awe, still trying to comprehend how this ex-pagan high priest and former warlord who has only known unspeakable violence his entire life, could be so beautifully transformed into an instrument of God's glory. As the apostle Paul said of the early church leaders regarding his own conversion, I can truly say, regarding Joshua, "And they glorified God in me" (Gal. 1:24).

BOJAN JANCIC

# PREFACE

This book is written to reveal the abundant grace, love, and mercy of our Father in Heaven to us His children. I feel so privileged to be called a child of the Most High God. It is an honor comparable to none. Words cannot express my gratitude to God, the Father of my Lord and Savior Jesus Christ, who made it possible for me to publish this testimony. Herein is the scripture fulfilled: "For with God nothing shall be impossible" (Luke 1:37 KJV). I am a living testimony of His Word. If I can be saved after all the atrocities I committed, then, dear reader, I urge you to resist the devil, for he will flee—and God will welcome you.

All I have written in this book is the truth, the whole truth, and nothing but the truth, no matter how shocking some of the words and situations are.

During the Liberian civil crisis, Liberians and the rest of the world referred to me as "General Butt Naked" because I fought completely nude. I had to fight "butt naked" because it was the demand of the spiritual force that empowered me. That is just one example of the distance Satan will go to humiliate a human being in the name of giving him or her power. Is that power worth the trauma, the mental torture, and depression that the devil dumps on you? Definitely not. He is a liar and the father of lies (see John 8:44).

My purpose in writing this book is not to paint a portrait of myself, but to set the record straight and refute any other publication intended to make irrelevant my new birth, lifestyle, and freedom. The scriptures declare that if any person be in Christ, that person is a new creature (see 2 Cor. 5:17). I am new indeed.

After you read my testimony, please say the sinner's prayer at the end of the book and let the Holy Spirit of the Most High God take control in every area of your life. As you surrender to Him, your life will never be the same again.

God bless you.

## Chapter 1

# THE SARPO-KRAHN TRIBE

I was born into the Sarpo-Krahn people, one of the Kwa-speaking tribes in Sinoe County in southeastern Liberia, in Western Africa. The ancestors of our tribe were warriors who believed in conquest. After conquering their opponents, they made them relinquish their sovereignty by entering into a treaty with them. The reason for this treaty was spiritual.

These ancient warriors understood the power in spoken words, and held it in high esteem. They believed they could be bewitched or cursed if the defeated opponents themselves did not verbally renounce their authority over their people and properties before turning them over to their captors. Thus, the victors led their defeated opponents through the following declarations to nullify the spiritual control of the land's gods and turn it over to their own gods:

1. Agree that the gods of our fathers that empowered us to conquer you shall have access into

the hidden places of your gods, and even if you go there to take refuge, we are entitled to bring you back.

2.  Agree that the blood and water we used in conquering you and your land have nullified the blood and water you used in founding this land and its preservation.

3.  Agree that you will be our servants and everything that belongs to you by nature and achievements belongs to us.

4.  Agree that our blood and water used in conquering you have nullified the blood and water that was used in getting your crops and livestock.

5.  Agree that our blood and water used in conquering you have nullified the blood and water that your parents used in bearing you.

6.  Agree that our blood and water used in conquering you have nullified the blood and water you used in bearing your children now and unborn.

7.  Agree that as of now you shall come under the gods of our fathers and it shall render you useless if the blood and water from your body ever cease responding to us in the affirmative.

Because of this tradition, our ancestors made it their whole purpose never to be defeated, and built the tribal culture around ensuring that the tribe was always growing braver and stronger. One of the ways they did this was by giving headship of the tribe, not to the eldest, but to the strongest. Every year, the head would have to defend his position and prove his strength in an annual fight, a fight decided by wounds, broken bones, and even death.

## THE PEACEFUL SON

From his youth, one of the sons of the Krahn tribe was not interested in fighting for land or headship, and always managed to escape the annual fight. Though he received insults for his position, he did not change it. Finally, he decided to leave. He and his immediate families set out to find a suitable place to settle, a place that would not interest or threaten his kinsmen.

The family eventually arrived at the Atlantic Ocean, and from there they journeyed along the coast until they found a plain land in which to build a settlement—the site of present-day Greenville, Liberia. They multiplied as the years passed, and after about seventy years, the family had grown into a multitude now known as Sarpo or Sarpo-Krahn.[1]

Greenville was established with the peaceful spirit of the Sarpo father who did not believe in rivalry and conquest. In those days, even escaping slaves sought refuge in Greenville, confident that their masters would not seek them in a city so far from the regions valuable to warriors. Up to this day, the city accepts every tribe and people.

## MISSIONARIES ARRIVE IN GREENEVILLE

One morning, the inhabitants of Greenville woke to see a large object on the Atlantic Ocean. They began to gather each morning and evening on the seashore to look at it. Some said it was a water cow, some a water elephant, and others a house that the water had carried from somewhere. Each day the object increased in size, and at night produced lights very unlike the fire they used. When the object drew nearer, the natives discerned moving objects on the ship, which they finally realized as people—people with a different color complexion and who waved to them whenever they came out to the shore. This frightened the natives. They began to make a plan to meet these intruders.

Finally, the day came when a lifeboat arrived onshore carrying a team appointed to meet the land dwellers. As they disembarked, the strong faces of the natives surrounded them, each holding a spear. But the smiles and innocent faces of the visitors, along with their ready compliance to do whatever was asked of them, quickly discouraged the natives. It became clear, particularly when the visitors began offering them sachets of food, that they had not come to fight, but to fellowship.

After a week, the elders of the settlement decided these visitors were harmless and welcomed them as good people. As a matter of fact, they were missionaries bringing the gospel of Jesus Christ. The missionaries pitched their tents beside the seashore and set about their first task: learning the tribe's language and culture. The female missionaries began working with the women and the male missionaries did the same with the men. They worked on the farm, went on hunting trips, learned traditional music, and bathed and ate with the natives.

After two years, the missionaries had mastered the dialect and began to share the gospel, convincing the natives of the salvation plan of God for humankind through Christ Jesus. The only problem was that the Sarpo fathers misunderstood the missionaries on one particular point, which later brought disaster on them. They got the idea that because God left His home in heaven and came to the home of the missionaries, and the missionaries left their home to come to them, therefore they must also leave their homes to let others know the Good News. After the missionaries went home, the natives made up their minds to spread the message to their brethren. They left Greenville with all their people and went back to the homeland from which their peace-seeking father had brought them.

Due to the large numbers of women and children, the journey lasted about two months. When they arrived, their tribal brothers could not recognize them. Though they sounded like their brothers, they could not be sure they were, for their intonation had slightly changed. This left their brothers with one option: to use the special traditional greetings. However, the Sarpo fathers could not respond because such traditional greetings were expressions of war. The tradition was that the person greeting would hit his brother, who would then hit back, and this began an aggressive wrestling match. After that, they exchanged pleasantries and showered praises on themselves:

"I'm the devil," says one.

"I am the first to strike," responds the other.

"I am complete."

"The child that has no mate."

"The one enthroned."

These warring acts were among the reasons the Sarpo father had left for a strange land in the first place. Moreover, the gospel preached by the missionaries had confirmed and deepened their value for peace. When the leader of the Sarpo fathers and his entourage could not respond to the Krahn greetings, they were proclaimed enemies. Seeing their numbers, the Krahn fathers released their best fighters upon the travel-weary, peaceful Sarpo families. The Krahn injured and killed nearly 90 percent of the men, along with many women and children. Those who survived were scattered into the bush.

## ENTER NYA-GHE-A-WEH

Eventually, the Sarpo managed to regroup and plan their journey back to their coastal home. In those days, travelers did not sleep on the plain for fear of wild animals. They would find a tree, a big rock, or any high structure where they could sleep safely. One night, after many days of travel, they came to a huge rock where they decided to pass the night.

The strong men among them stayed awake to keep watch. In the middle of the night, a wind arose, blowing the trees back and forth for almost two hours. A cloud of fear and heaviness grew over the men, causing all but one, Saydee, to fall asleep. An unknown voice came strongly to Saydee's ears, saying, "The warrior without equal."

Saydee sat frozen for some time, but finally stirred and quietly whispered, "Who is it?"

"The one whose bosom you have come under," the voice replied.

He pondered over this strange voice, which had described him as a warrior without equal. How could that be true? He had just lost almost all his people. Surely this voice was mocking him. After a while, he broke the silence again by asking, "You have not told me what you want from me and I cannot see you. Will you keep talking to me from the dark?"

"What do I want from you?" the voice echoed. "I need your friendship, which will enable me to help you and your people. I will not speak with you in the dark once you understand me and know that I am here to help."

In that moment, Saydee realized that the men keeping watch with him were no longer speaking. Frightened, he called for them in the darkness, asking, "Did you call me 'warrior'"?

"Yes, you are a warrior," said the mysterious voice. "A great one too. This is why everyone else has fallen into a sleeping spell except you. Moreover, you are going to humble those people, the ones you called brothers, the very ones you are running from. You are going to walk on their blood."

"What! I must be talking with a god!" Saydee whispered.

"You have rested under the shelter that will remain till your last generation," said the voice.

As the old man heard these last words fade away, he shouted, "Don't go! I have not understood some things yet."

"I am not gone from you," the voice replied. "Meet me behind this rock tonight, and I will tell you everything you need to know."

Thus did Nya-ghe-a-weh first speak to old man Saydee, who afterward ran to the rest of the men and woke them up to explain his experience. "He said I should meet him behind the rock tonight, but how are we going to do this? If I should meet him tonight, we will spend the entire day here again."

"Yes," said one of them, "if you believe that he is a god, then he might want to help us. It is worth spending another day here." They agreed to stay, spent the day hunting for food, and returned to the rock when night fell.

## NYA-GHE-A-WEH'S EMPOWERMENT AND DECEPTION

Saydee went behind the rock as the voice had instructed him. After about twenty minutes of walking around the rock, he asked himself, "Where am I going to meet him?"

"You are welcome, my brave and strong warrior!" said the strange voice to Saydee.

Counting his words and stuttering, Saydee replied, "I came as discussed. But I didn't know what to call you."

"Nya-ghe-a-weh is what you and anyone after you shall call me. I'm going to empower you to take revenge for the massacre your people suffered in the hands of your Krahn brothers. Take this talisman (a catlike animal tail, with carrot shell) and touch all of your able men with this. The ones who remain awake will be empowered with strange fighting skills. They will be able to fight like any fighting animal, including birds. They will disappear and reappear. Not only that, metals will not be able to penetrate them. Let them follow you. Now stretch out your left hand!"

When the old man did as he was told, a cutlass[2] entered his hand from nowhere.

"Keep your hand up and don't allow it to fall," Nya-ghe-a-weh commanded the old man.

Standing there, the old man began to shout and shiver as he endeavored to keep his hand raised with the cutlass. He quickly became soaked in sweat, as it was not an easy task. Then suddenly, power charged his limbs.

Early the next morning, he returned to his brothers with the shout of a warrior. The rest of his brothers were all astonished when they saw him. They could tell from his countenance that something strange had taken over him. He requested that all the strong men be summoned so that he could carry out the instruction of Nya-ghe-a-weh. As he touched them with the talisman, all but thirteen of the men fell asleep. When the talisman touched these thirteen, they began sneezing unusually. After this sneezing had gone on for a while, they raised the warrior's shout and took off running through the thick bush behind the old man Saydee.

After this dramatic act preparing the men for battle (which holds today as a ritual), Saydee sent the thirteen men ahead of him to begin their revenge mission against the Krahn, saying, "Go and subdue anyone who rises against you. You shall return untouched."

He went back to the rest of the men and encouraged them to take care of themselves, make provision for food, and take special care of the wounded men among them. Then he bid them goodbye and promised that he and the thirteen men would return.

Then mysteriously, though he had set off behind them, the thirteen men heard the old man Saydee ahead of them on the trail, calling them to follow him as he led them to the battle. They got to the land of their kinsmen the next day, but waited around the town for nightfall before attacking. When the entire town was asleep, Saydee was mysteriously led to the houses of the strongest men, in descending rank. He beheaded each of them.

## THE GREAT PAYBACK

Early in the morning, there was confusion and lamentation all over the town. "Evil has befallen us," people cried. "Great father, didn't you remind the gods to watch over us as they did for you?"

"Leave our fathers to rest with your vain cries!" Saydee announced. He was perched in a tall palm tree in the middle of the town. *"You* have chosen that we waste the blood of our fathers' house. They are going to watch us continue the bloodbath. You asked for it, and now you must get it."

He commanded the thirteen men to go after villagers and make sure they lost as much blood as they had shed. Shouting, the men jumped down from a huge cotton tree in the middle of town and began thrusting spears into people. The men of the town noticed that the men fighting them were few, so they decided to come together and fight back. However, they discovered that their Sarpo brothers could change into all kinds of creatures during the battle—flying from tree to tree, disappearing and reappearing. Seeing these warriors, the Krahn fathers then realized that they had murdered their own brothers. They signaled for peace, crying, "We are sorry, brothers! We are wrong. We will take the blame for everything, both the blood that we wasted then and our own blood now." Saydee called off his warriors, and the war stopped at once.

Every man, woman, and child gathered at the town square to pay tribute to the lost souls. There was a long period of silence as the Krahn fathers waited for the conquerors, the Sarpo fathers, to pronounce the covenant for them, the victims, to repeat. Finally, Saydee broke the silence and said, "We should not be considered as victors in this battle, because we are from the same household. Both parties are victims, because we killed ourselves. If we were to measure the blood wasted a few weeks ago, we would find it equal to the blood of your own people shed today.

"We do not understand why you did not believe us in the first place. You know well that none of the Kwa-speaking tribes around here will be subject to another person, because they got to where they are by their own strength and not by birthright. But it is not so with us. Our father told us that we came from you. We are the descendants of one of your brothers who refused to fight for the right of headship. Our father refused to continue the tradition of his ancestors and left to find a land that would be free from war. We were living peacefully and happily till our peaceful spirit attracted foreigners who came to show us true and good reasons for living. Our founding father died a peaceful death, at a very reasonable age, too.

"He always told us that every man should recognize his origin, as that is the only way he will appreciate who he is. He then told us about you, our people of origin. He begged us to recognize you and encouraged us to identify with you anytime you need us. Our father established it in our hearts that we should never see ourselves as greater than you, and that we should share with you anything that seems good to us. This is why we were led to come and share the things our foreign friends gave to us. But see what it has turned out to be. However, you are our elders. Whatever you want us to do now, we will do."

Saydee bowed to them and asked them to take over. For a long time, they were silent, looking at one another and weeping. The eldest stepped in and thanked Saydee for listening to his father and obeying his wishes. "Not many sons will obey their father's wishes, but you are different. Please allow us to withdraw to reach a consensus. We will join you later."

When they returned, the eldest brought a plate of kola nuts and pepper, signifying peace, brotherliness, and friendship among the entire Kwa-speaking tribes. The eldest began his speech, "We are truly sorry for everything we have caused you. The elders have reached an agreement for all the troubles and the blood wasted. We will not share them with you. We are fully responsible and will bear the expected calamity. You did not take us as victims, but we want to know the god you worship, the god that has given you such powers. We are not denouncing our fathers' gods, but we want to worship the gods your fathers left with you. We agree that you are our brothers and you came from us as your father said. We agree to identify with you anytime and in anything.

"But we want to ask you for one favor, and please do not let us down. We do not want you to go far away from us again. You have finished our warriors, and other tribes will soon take over us once they notice. We will need your help at any moment. The only problem is that the blood we have shed is too much and cannot go unnoticed, so there is no way we can live together in the same town. Therefore, we will use this big mountain as our boundary. You should stay on that side where you came from, while we stay on this side."

"Truly, we cannot ignore the blood we wasted among ourselves," Saydee agreed. He accepted the request of his Krahn fathers, and asked them to embrace each other in appreciation and acceptance of their reunion. Thereafter, they set off for the journey back to the big rock where they had left their families, bringing with them livestock they received as gifts from their Krahn kinsmen. Saydee and the fighting men returned to the big rock with sad expressions on their faces. They did not look like people who had conquered their opponents. However, the rest of the people were happy, because Saydee and the other men came back from the battle without injury. They celebrated by dancing and singing, and stopped at one point to hear Saydee tell the story of the battle.

## THE COVENANT INITIATION

As night fell, Nya-ghe-a-weh's strange presence induced Saydee to dance around the big rock.

"Didn't I tell you that you would be my warriors?" Nya-ghe-a-weh said.

"Yes, you said so; and your shelter is truly great. My tribe and I wish to stay under it forever," Saydee said.

"My shelter is already yours, my great warrior. You, your people, and your generations unborn will benefit from it. My request is that you and your generation remain faithful to me and pass me on to your future generations."

Saydee declared, "We are now under your control. Only you know what we need to do if we will remain under your shelter forever."

Nya-ghe-a-weh, quick to respond, said, "First, you need to know that this rock is my throne. It has been kept sacred until you came with your multitude and defiled it. You will bring your people from that side of my throne and take them farther down this side. You can build your homes and live right here with me as long as you wish. First thing tomorrow, you will move to the side allocated to you and barricade the side between you and me. *You will then cleanse my throne with the blood of four of your female babies.*"

"Consider all you said done," Saydee said. He did exactly what Nya-ghe-a-weh commanded him to do.

Afterward, Nya-ghe-a-weh said, "I love you and your people so much, and I will not allow your people to leave this world like other tribes. I will prepare a place behind this rock where you rested on your arrival here. I shall make it a place of eternal rest. I will take all my faithful ones from this world when their time of rest comes. I know they need to rest, and I will have them stay in this specially prepared place. I will make sure you have access to your children when you are resting with me, and they shall have access to you as well. But I need you to send ahead nine of your able young men who are still virgins to be your servants whenever you or any of the faithful come to rest."[3]

Saydee met with the second demand, killing nine young men, just as he had the four infant girls.

In response, Nya-ghe-a-weh said, "Tomorrow I am going to take you to my place, where I will formally empower you to be my chief priest. You will be there until I am completely through with you, and it will take us a little time. The men who were able to stand when you returned in my power from the battle will be the elders of the tribe as from now on. When you return to them, you will still need them to be heads over the people, as you will be a god to them all. Your presence before the ordinary men and women could harm them, so those elders will stand as emissaries to your people. When you come tomorrow, you are to bring an infant between the age of one day and three years for a covenant between the tribe and me. Tell your people to start a feast that will continue until your return."

When Saydee came the next day with the child, Nya-ghe-a-weh was standing at the gate of the fence to meet him. Saydee turned the child over. Holding the child, Nya-ghe-a-weh asked Saydee to repeat everything he said. "Everything said in this place is accepted by me and my tribe.

Everything accepted shall be implemented by my tribe to the letter. If I, my tribe's men now, or the generation yet unborn go against any of the things I accept here today, all the unborn generations shall not reach the age of this innocent child with whom we are making this covenant in this great shelter."

The old man recited every word spoken by Nya-ghe-a-weh, and they entered into covenant. Then Nya-ghe-a-weh gave the old man his laws.

"My identity and everything about me will never be revealed to anyone by you or other priests who will come after you, because only my priest will be given the ability to see me. *My priesthood shall be limited to your quarter* (the Julukon quarter) and no member of your quarter will ever eat kola nut or play with it." (This law was intended to make the tribe selfish. According to the traditions of the Kwa ethnic group, the giving and accepting of kola nuts is the sign of approving a friendship or a visit. Having nothing to do with kola nuts meant we would have no dealing with the entire Kwa ethnic group and would keep to ourselves.)

"Every member of the Sarpo tribe belongs to me. In fact, any person I choose to serve me as my priest should count himself favored. Every child born into this tribe must be dedicated to me, and I will thereafter register the child in the coven for full protection. If any man from this tribe dies and you wish to be in contact with him, you will shave the dead man's hair and bring it to my coven.

"As I have found you worthy and chosen you to be my priest, nothing shall change that. I will always choose my priest when the former one passes on to glory, and every priest will make his sacrifice to me according to the power and influence he wants. If you keep my laws and immortalize me in the heart of your children and generation yet unborn, nothing shall stand before you. You will represent me in this physical world, and remain my delight forever."

The tribe increased, and Nya-ghe-a-weh was worshiped and adored as their god, they trusted him as well for protection and even for provision. From time to time, they had one priest or the other. My tribesmen do not believe that their fathers die, but that they go to join their fathers if they were faithful. They hold this concept very sacred, and it contributed to their brave nature.

## THE PATH TO BECOMING A PRIEST

As mandated by Nya-ghe-a-weh, the priestly mantle falls only on a first male child from the Julukon quarter. For this reason, every Julukon first male child is trained as a warrior and must pass through all the traditional practices and observe all the precepts of Nya-ghe-a-weh carefully. After the ruling priest is "taken by the fathers," the elders will take him to the sacred place in the forest and wait for Nya-ghe-a-weh to select the next priest.

When he turns eight, each first male child begins to sit and contribute to every matter in his father's house. His father will not make any major decision without his consent. He must be at every general tribal meeting where the tribe's progress is discussed, and air his views on any issue being deliberated upon in the town square or at the elders' secret closet. These privileges train first sons to attain wisdom and understanding of the issues pertaining to the tribe and their way of life.

According to Julukon precept, courtesy demands that every male child fends for himself as soon as he is eight years old. He is made a laughingstock if he still eats from his mother's soup pot after he turns eight, so he learns to fish and hunt to prepare his own soup every day. Fathers teach their first sons to hunt with guns and traps on land, water, and trees, and to farm—to fell big trees, burn the farm, fence it against crop-destroying animals, and so forth. The elders strongly believe this is the only way to make the child mature for the priestly task. They believe hard work will make the boy successful, as he will have no time to play or talk with others. They believe it will make him independent and self-reliant, able to make decisions without the influence of his peers. They believe that by spending the day in the forest, he won't be interested in distractions to the priesthood. They also believe so much solitude will encourage the boy to be a thinker.

Once a father is convinced that his first son is mature, he is respected among his peers and nobody interrupts him while he is talking. But if a first son is not turning out to be what is expected of a first son, he is called "useless" and other names of ridicule. If he tries to defend himself, he is mocked even more. Everyone in the tribe thinks it is better for the man whose first son dies or is disabled, and is thus disqualified from the priesthood, than for the man whose first son is immature. The child who is not responding to the training could still be selected by Nya-ghe-a-weh, but doing so would threaten the traditional and cultural foundation built by the tribe's ancestors. The fear of a bad and weak priest who could pollute the land and hinder the visitation of their forefathers on a yearly basis inspires hatred for the fathers who cannot groom their sons. The fathers of weak boys are also called useless men. To avoid the stigma of having a weak son and show that they hold the tradition of their ancestors above their family, most fathers kill sons viewed to be incapable.

## ENDNOTES

1. There have been controversies in understanding the difference between the Sarpo and Krahn tribes. Sarpo is one of the ethnic groups among the different Krahn groups. Others include Tchein, Kuanibo, Gborbo, and Gbarbo. The peculiar history of the Sarpo clan has projected it as a tribe on its own, and for this reason politicians from the clan are agitating to have their own county. The Sarpo clan grew into six different sub-clans: Kabadeh, Nimupoh, Putu, Seekon, Juarzon, and Wedjah. My parents are from Kabadeh, the seat of the ancient god of my forefathers known as Nya-ghe-a-weh, whose control and influence has spread over the entire Kwa-speaking regions of Liberia and Cote d'Ivoire (Ivory Coast).

2. A cutlass is a short, curved sword.

3. This is where the notion came from that the priest and other fathers do not die.

## Chapter 2

# FAMILY TIES

Nnawyilee was the oldest uncle of my paternal grandfather. He was the angel of our tribe from the civilized world, bringing great change in the history of the Sarpo tribe.

After many years, the Sarpo men went back to claim their coastal land at Greenville. There they were confronted with stiff opposition by a Kru chief who wanted to be a governor over his own empire. However, the Sarpo fathers fought back. The battle over Greenville lasted for more than five years, until the Kru chief finally sought help from the empire from which he had originally broken away. That governor gave him single-barreled guns (a very modern weapon then) and made him his commissioner over Greenville. Though the fight was not over for the Sarpo fathers, they were weakened and only went to war against the Kru once in a while.

Eventually, the governor felt the need to broker peace between both parties. Therefore he paid a courtesy visit to Sarpo land, though he did not accept their proposal to hand over

Greenville. The governor and his entire congress, particularly their dress, fascinated Nnawyilee, who was just in his teens at that time. He realized they came from a wonderful place.

Nnawyilee was actually a spoiled child. His father had six sons before him, but they had all died when a wild lioness attacked them to retrieve her babies, which the boys had brought from their cave to play with at the farm. For this reason, Nnawyilee's father never allowed him to go to the forest with his friends. This earned him their mockery, so he was always found among girls.

When the governor visited the tribe, Nnawyilee, bored and dissatisfied with his life, decided to run away. He snuck into the governor's entourage back to Greenville and was captivated by the reception that met the governor there. He was moved by the governor's speech asking his people to be peaceful with their neighbors and embrace civilization. He was attracted to the idea that in civilization, legitimacy was not determined by might but by the rule of law. The governor told them about his visit to another empire, which had a formal educational system to inculcate this civilization. He then announced that he had made provisions for this system to be established in the empire's capital town, Sass Town. He explained that this new system would make the current traditional education unnecessary.

Nnawyilee decided to follow the governor on to Sass Town. He saw that Greenville and its people were not very different from his homeland and his people, and he wanted to learn more about this new education. Sure enough, when he came to Sass Town he was privileged to be among the first natives to benefit from Western education when it was first introduced there.

The education was free for almost ten years. When American Liberians took over from the missionaries, fees were introduced.

Nnawyilee could not afford to pay his fees, so he decided to return home. His father was happy to see him again, and told him of the demise of Nnawyilee's mother. According to his father, his mother died from the shock of losing her only hope, Nnawyilee, after already having to grieve the death of her six sons in the carnivorous claws and jaws of the lioness.

"Oh Father!" Nnawyilee exclaimed. "I am so sorry I caused Mama's death." He cried, clinging to his father, and could not forgive himself.

"No, my son, don't do this to yourself," said his father, trying to calm him. "It has already happened. Don't kill yourself now that I need you so dearly."

"When did she die, Father?" Nnawyilee asked.

"Three years ago."

"Was she able to have any other child?"

"No."

"So it means that you have been in this house all alone ever since Mama died?"

"No, son. You have not stopped crying, so I have not been able to tell you other things. Your mother requested her death from the fathers. In that regard, she was privileged to know her time was come. A few weeks before her death, she brought your aunt's daughter to bear children in her stead, though I have yet to make her my wife. Your mother thought her name was forgotten, not knowing you were alive somewhere. So you see how your coming back home has helped to reconcile some things."

Preventing Nnawyilee from seeking other reasons to blame himself, he held his hands and said, "Come with me, my son. Let me take you to your mother's grave to let her know you are here. But promise me you will not cry, for your mother will not like to see you crying."

"Let us go, Father. I will not cry. Take me to Mama."

After they returned from his mother's grave, his father asked him to explain his sudden disappearance from home.

"I was ignorant, Father," Nnawyilee said. He said he had been fascinated by the attire of the governor and his entourage. "It was good that I left. The love you and Mama showered on me made me useless to the lifestyle in this village. My peers would not allow me to sit with them because I could not do things like them. Now I have discovered a different lifestyle—a lifestyle that is taking over the whole world. And I will be a light to my father's land and tribe."

"What are you saying, my son?" Nnawyilee's father asked in excitement and curiosity. Without waiting for a response, he rose up and started dancing around the little hut and pointing to the place known to be his father's resting place. "You mean my own son will soon be a light to his father's land and people in the cause of this new dispensation you just related to me?"

"Yes, Father."

"I think your aunt's food will be ready by now. Let us eat and get to some of the elders to inform them about the good news you brought to our fathers' land." Nnawyilee's father explained how the aunty who served them food had been good to him. "She has indeed helped me bear the death of your mother. Let us go and see some of the influential elders. Hopefully they can convince the other elders to let you to relate your new discovery at the next general tribal gathering."

Nnawyilee's explanation impressed all the elders, and Nnawyilee was given permission to brief the elders and tribal quorum about his education at the general tribal meeting. The boy and his father were elated, and could not wait for the meeting. Nnawyilee was especially excited to look respectable before his peers who had looked down on him. As the day came closer, Nnawyilee could be seen with a broad smile on his face, an expression of victory over his past humiliation.

On the day of the general meeting, other issues were deliberated before they called on Nnawyilee to address the people. When his turn came, Nnawyilee prostrated himself before the chief elder. "I greet you my elders. I cannot speak to the ones who represent the fathers without the grace of the fathers."

The chief elder touched Nnawyilee with his staff and told him to stand up in assurance that the elders were solidly behind him. He urged him to speak on.

"I thank the fathers so much for their willingness to protect this land with everything they have and for managing this generation toward the path of the elders. I strongly believe that the fathers are proud of their children, who are our fathers today, because they did not lead our generation astray in the task of protecting our great land and our convictions."

The elders nodded with approval as Nnawyilee continued, "I think it is a privilege and special blessing from our forefathers for a child like me to refresh my fathers' memories about the history of our great tribe. I choose to use the word 'refresh' because the fathers know the history better than I do. Hence I will depend on them for correction when I go wrong.

"We were told that our founding father was a very intelligent man whose reasoning was not common in his time. He saw no reason in fighting his own brothers for land while there were many lands unoccupied; and because he never wanted to fight with any other tribe, he moved his immediate family members to an environment he felt would be favorable. He preferred a land far away in order not to attract other tribes. The peaceful spirit of our father affected the land so much that it became a safe place for escaped slaves and refugees from oppressive conquerors."

Nnawyilee stopped to observe the elders and make sure they were still following in agreement. Then he said, "The numerical growth of the tribe was great as a result of intermarriage."

The elders tried to digest this statement. They looked at each other in amazement. The thrust of Nnawyilee's account seemed to be reminding the elders of their peaceful background and urging the need to suppress anything in the contrary. This emphasis was almost misconstrued, but the elders soon mended their differences.

Nnawyilee continued his account, describing the massacre their fathers suffered at the hands of their barbaric Krahn brothers and comparing it to the new order in Greenville suppressing the Sarpo tribe. As he spoke, he won the heart of his father, who wished his wife was still alive to witness the bravery of their son. His words created murmuring among the elders, until the presiding elder intervened and signaled for Nnawyilee to continue.

Nnawyilee concluded by delivering his opinion that his kinsmen couldn't give up their land in Greenville for the reason that their forefathers were buried there. "We can't give up. We'll fight, but this time with a different method—the method the foreigners brought to our forefathers, which is the very method the Kru and other empires are bragging about today. This method is like a weapon, greater than the spears and arrows our forefathers left behind for us."

At first, the warriors thought Nnawyilee was speaking of the single-barreled guns that were shot at them in Greenville, and thought Nnawyilee had brought some for them. But of course he was speaking about preferring Western education over their traditional education, in which boys are groomed to become inhuman. He described a time when issues would not be decided by strength but by the rule of law, and only the educated would benefit. He explained further by telling them about things he heard from the governor and things he discovered while in school. He narrated his experiential knowledge in school. To him, the new Western education was a new dispensation that should replace the old method.

## MODERN EDUCATION RESISTED

Nnawyilee's conclusion put the elders in disarray. Many of them were in support of his opinion. The elders appreciated him for his boldness, but cautioned the people that no one should take action until the elders met to conclude on the matter.

Two days later, the priest, as spokesman of the god, came into the town to deliver the verdict of Nya-ghe-a-weh on Nnawyilee's speech. He said, "The god is not satisfied that you have decided to leave the traditions of your fathers and accept a new one. The god sent me to warn you that this should not be heard anymore among you, unless you want to choose between him and your so-called new culture." (Nya-ghe-a-weh and other black witches know that education, wealth, and exposure to other cultures are serious weapons against them, though every weapon has to be taught before it can be properly utilized. Any change that may possibly awaken the consciousness of people under the tutelage of the devil and his cohorts, including Nya-ghe-a-weh, poses the highest threat to the dark world.)

After this verdict on Nnawyilee's educational renaissance, the elders summoned a prompt meeting, in which they resolved to warn parents sternly not to support any of their children who may give value to Nnawyilee's philosophy of education, lest they face the wrath of Nya-ghe-a-weh.

Nnawyilee was banished from the town, but he felt no loss. He admonished his father to go into the woman his mother betrothed to him and have more children. The old man did according to his son's counsel and had three other children, two boys and a girl. He christened the first son Blahyi, who became my paternal grandfather. His daughter was named Portai, and she became the mother of many grandchildren. She was the first tutor the elders sent to me because she carried the history of the tribe. Charlie, the last of them, singlehandedly pioneered education in Sarpo.

My grandfather took over his father's name because his father became a drunkard, being unable to condone the insolence of the elders' decision. My grandfather Blahyi did everything within his means to give his late father a befitting burial. My grandfather became the toast of his family members, including Nnawyilee, my grandfather's eldest brother.

## THE SECRET CAMPAIGN FOR EDUCATION

Despite his banishment, Nnawyilee managed to sneak into Sarpo on occasion. Whenever he did so, he encouraged the young boys to pursue the educational opportunity in Sass Town. Some began to escape to Sass Town for education, but the romance soon died when they were unable to settle their bills. Worse, they knew could not go back home after having disregarded the elders' counsel. Eventually, the elders persuaded the new priest to appease the god and mix justice with mercy. The god hearkened to the people and the law was amended so that it only applied to every first male child (retained for the priesthood), permitting other Sarpo people to pursue their ambition outside the town.

Charlie, Nnawyilee's youngest brother, grew up and left to join Nnawyilee in Sass Town. When Charlie fully understood the importance of education, he began luring young people into it. He encouraged them to work and bring their products to Sass Town for sale, thereby raising money for their education. Charlie set up a program for his only sister and brother's children, employing some and using the proceeds of their work to service the others' educational ambitions.

## THE BIRTH OF MY FATHER

Blahyi, my grandfather, commanded respect for his hard work. He was one of the primary food providers for the tribe in his time. My grandfather married my grandmother, Cherfani. My father, Kwetii, was born, followed by two girls, Waihnyonoh and Wehyi, and last by a boy my grandfather named after his elder brother, Nnawyilee. My father was trained as a first son according to the tradition and did powerful things, winning prizes as the greatest hunter on two successive occasions. He once delivered his aunt's son, George Falley, from the paws of a leopard.

My father's younger brother, Nnawyilee, grew and started school. Nnawyilee was very brilliant, and since he had every support and encouragement, he went far and fast in his learning. My father took full responsibility for his brother's education. Nothing could compare or share his love for his brother. He worked and made sure his younger brother lacked nothing. Whenever the students came home to Kabadeh on vacation, they told the tribe what education would soon turn the world into. Their reports made my father do anything in his means to support his brother's education and life, with the hope that Nnawyilee would one day become the first governor of his people.

Nnawyilee became the first to complete high school among the Sarpo people, and set a day to return home and celebrate his graduation. His father, old man Blahyi, and his brother Kwetii (my father) were ready to make that day the most memorable of his lifetime. The entire town was invited to the party, and all the best singers and dancers were prepared to entertain.

Nnawyilee brought some classmates and friends with him from Sass Town for the celebration. The ceremony started in earnest with melodious songs and dances. Nnawyilee came to my father's house so he could accompany him to the ceremony at the town square. My father took Nnawyilee by the hand and led him to the seat already prepared in the midst of the large crowd. My father welcomed everybody and told them to enjoy everything at the party, encouraging them to request any animal for the feast. There was noise all over the crowd, calling for different kinds of animals. They finally agreed on an antelope.

As he left the gathering for his house to prepare the antelope, men rushed after him with his brother, who had blood gushing out of his nose. My father tried talking to his brother, but the only thing he could hear from him was, "They asked me what I would do with the so-called education now."

"Who told you that, Nnawyilee? Talk to me! Who told you so?"

Nnawyilee looked straight into my father's eyes and said, "I will not make it. But please do me a favor by establishing our father's name among the educated people."

"Yes, but Nnawyilee, tell me first who told you what you said before now?" He did everything to get his brother to talk, but to no avail. The death of my father's brother hurt him so much that nothing in the town interested him anymore.

# MY FATHER TO APPEASE HIS BROTHER'S SPIRIT

When my father learned that the death of his brother had discouraged the people in support of education, he decided to go against the traditionalists. My father stopped going to the usual warriors' meetings. When his Uncle Charlie came to town, my father told him that he was no longer interested in the whole tradition. Moreover, he wished to please the spirit of his brother by leaving the town for school.

Uncle Charlie was troubled by my father's decision, as it violated the law of the tribe prohibiting eldest sons to be educated, and denied his responsibility to uphold the tribe's traditions and remain eligible for the priesthood. He was not sure my father really meant what he was saying. But he did not want to say things to further frustrate him, so Uncle Charlie told my father that admission into school could only begin with the next session, and assured him he would secure admission for him by that time. Uncle Charlie then appealed to my father to handle traditional issues with utmost care. My father agreed to do so, but also begged his uncle to arrange for his education.

When Uncle Charlie left Kabadeh, he carried other young boys along to school in Sass Town. When my father found out, he became furious and frustrated, taking it as a sign that his uncle did not mean to help him get into the school. He took his gun and went hunting, killing lots of animals, which he took to Sass Town to sell. He made up his mind that he would not allow his uncle to have any hand in his schooling, but in the end, he could not support himself in Sass Town. Later, Uncle Charlie helped resolve their differences and assisted him in starting his education. My father was very clever and learned quickly.

Uncle Charlie was like a son to Mr. Been (and was even known as Charlie Been), who was more or less the county superintendent. Mr. Been also adopted my father and called him Joseph Been. It was the Been name that my father used to gain employment into the Ministry of Finance. At that time, Liberian natives could not go so far in the government, but my father worked with Finance Minister Steven A. Tolbert (brother to President William R. Tolbert Jr.) as his special accountant. My father became the clerk to Mr. Been when Uncle Charlie left to be the messenger (a very big post at the time) to Juarzon District. When Mr. Been was posted to Sinoe, my father moved to Monrovia to live there.

Back in Kabadeh, my grandfather Blahyi was being troubled by the elders because of my father. The reputation he had built over the years as a food provider had diminished immediately when my father left. He dared not say a word among his peers, but old man Blahyi sent messages begging my father to come and see them. My father hid behind flimsy excuses, though he assured his father that he was still abreast of the traditional rites, and if his forefathers needed him, he would contribute whatever was obligatory. When the old man related his son's response to the elders, they called him a fool and said his son took after him. Their skepticism was borne out of the fact that it was not the first time that the Blahyi family had caused problems for the tribe.

My father joined his uncle, Charlie, in supporting the young people in their academic pursuits, thanks to his income as special accountant to Steven Tolbert. Every two months, my grandfather visited Charlie and my father in Monrovia. Each time he related how the elders were pressuring him about his son and reminding him that he, old as he was, could be called upon by the forefathers at any time.

# THE PRIESTLY MANTLE FALLS UPON MY FATHER

When the ruling priest finally died, the elders told my grandfather that if he did not bring his son, he could not stay in Kabadeh with them. My grandfather traveled to Juarzon, where Uncle Charlie was, and demanded that he go with him to get my father from Monrovia. The two brothers arrived in Monrovia early in the morning and went directly to my father's house, only to learn from his neighbors that my father had not been seen for almost two days. They decided to go to their cousin, old man Sarkpeh,[1] who lived by Lynch Street in a community called Sohni, and see if my father was there. Sure enough, he was.

When my father saw his father and his uncle, he started speaking with a very sad face. "Uncle Charlie, I am glad you came with him. I am very happy."

"What has happened to you, my son?" his father asked.

"I was disgraced the day before yesterday in my office, right before my secretary," my father answered.

"What, were you beaten?" Uncle Charlie asked.

"No, I was not beaten. The forefathers have chosen me, and the priestly mantle fell on me as I sat at my desk."

Immediately, my grandfather requested a cup of water to give to my father, by which he could "spew from his mouth" what he had just said. My grandfather asked, "My son, how can you describe the call of the fathers as a disgrace? Do you know how many people in our land wish to be called?"

"No, big brother," explained Uncle Charlie. "You did not understand him. He was not talking about the forefathers' call being the disgrace, but the action in the presence of his colleagues and juniors who may not have understood what was going on." Then my grandfather understood.

Old man Sarkpeh came in to calm them. "The best thing to do is to get your son to go back home with you," he said. "He has been expressing fears that something bad could happen because of the way he left without visiting Kabadeh."

"But what is he afraid of?" Grandfather Blahyi remarked. "No wonder the elders said if I don't bring him I shouldn't return to the town."

"Is that so, Joseph?" Uncle Charlie asked, looking at my father and squeezing his shoulder, as they walked. "I don't think you should be afraid. The fathers must have had interest in you before choosing you, and if so, they will give you all the protection you need. But I am wondering whether or not they will accept a replacement, seeing as you left them a long time and will not be able to function effectively as expected."

At midnight, they got to Kabadeh. The elders were harsh and unsympathetic with them, because they had gathered all the other firstborn at the town square for almost one week, waiting for the one the forefathers preferred. However, Uncle Charlie, Grandfather Blahyi, and my father managed to tell the elders the details of how the mantle had fallen on my father, with all the proof needed. They were also quick to suggest that my father's first son, who would study the tradition from infancy to have the understanding my father did not have, serve as a possible replacement.

This idea sounded very funny in the ears of the elders. However, the elders did not control the decisions of Nya-ghe-a-weh; they only received and interpreted them. They consulted the oracles and it accepted the idea. This was no surprise—the oracles had to accept the idea, because my father's educational status and wealth posed a threat to the traditional priestly throne. Nya-ghe-a-weh also sent the elders to old man Jay Swen, priest to another god similar in power and rank to Nya-ghe-a-weh, to officiate the so-called "translation festival," which established my father as interim priest. Old man Jay Swen came and conducted all the ceremonies as Nya-ghe-a-weh directed. My father was asked to provide everything for the festival, which he did. Afterward, he returned to Monrovia and continued his normal life, though, at the caution of the elders, he decided to look for a partner to settle down with in order to provide the priest for his people.

My father could go to his homeland freely, and he did so at the end of every year and on important occasions. Between those occasions, the people were in dire need of a priest to bless crops, perform rites, and offer various cures. Whenever they sent for Jay Swen, he came on his own time, not theirs. The elders needed to have their own priest who would meet their needs on time. Several attempts were made by unscrupulous men to usurp the priesthood. They felt powerful, and were able to deceive the elders that the mantle from the god had fallen upon them. The elders, who had no business in rejecting or accepting a priest, sent these men to meet the oracles. Those who deceived the elders about being called to the priesthood met a sad end, stricken to death by Nya-ghe-a-weh.

## MY FATHER MARRIED

My father married Ma Saybah, a Lorma woman from Lofa County in the northern part of Liberia. The Lofians have their own traditional and cultural practices, primarily within the Poro and Sande secret societies, which are widespread throughout southeastern Liberia and Sierra Leone. The Poro and Sande are almost the same, but the Poro is limited to the men while the Sande is for the women. Ma Saybah was part of the Sande society and had a very influential rank. Ma Saybah had a daughter before meeting my father. My father did not hide anything from Ma Saybah concerning his Sarpo background, and when she gave birth to a male child she was so happy to know that her son would move into his father's position as the next priest. She named him Benedict, but my father christened him Nnawyilee after his late brother.

After six months, Ma Saybah brought a Zoe (headwoman) by the name of Korboi to initiate Benedict into the Poro society. Benedict was initiated as a spy by the Poro and was charged never to slack in identifying with his Poro family. There is usually food cooked from which every member must eat to qualify them into full Poro membership, but Benedict's food was packaged and brought from the Poro bush when he was about three years old. They took two days to get him to eat the special food.

My father loved Benedict because he was his only child then, and he looked like my father. My father was not sure he would have more children at his age. Every day, the fact that my father had to "take Benedict to the village" became harder for him. His wife, not understanding all the implications of this duty, urged him not to hold back the promised child from the tribe. So my father finally took Benedict to his hometown and turned him over to the elders for introduction to Nya-ghe-a-weh. However, the oracle rejected him, saying Benedict was from a mixed culture and already had the mark of the other culture. Out of frustration, Nya-ghe-a-weh placed a curse of inconsistency upon the innocent child, which to this day is affecting his life.

"This child won't be our priest, for he may trade the heritage that has been protected by our forefathers and passed on to us. You must bring another child to be our priest, as was promised," the elders announced to my father.

"But fathers," he replied, "I am already married and the customary law pertaining to marriage in the city won't permit me to have another wife. My wife is the only one I have to bring forth children. Could I adopt or arrange a child who is not necessarily my own blood?"

"Fool!" the chief elder responded, pointing to my father's face. "This family has always brought unto us additional worries. Listen to me! We are going to arrange a woman worthy to bring forth our next priest and you must bring forth a male child. The decision to leave her here in the village or carry her along with you to Monrovia is your business."

My father was relieved. The proposal met his satisfaction, for his first and only son would return with him to Monrovia and the would-be priest's mother would just be an arranged woman. He bowed before the elders. "As I am leaving for the city, I will be awaiting your usual call to fulfill all the rites that will be required."

"You are not going anywhere," they demanded in a sharp tone. "Go to your useless father's house and wait while we conclude this matter."

## MY MOTHER'S INVOLVEMENT

My mother, Elizabeth Pantoe, was already married with two children (Nelson and Harrison) when she was selected by the oracle to be my father's wife. Her mother (my maternal grandmother) was from the Nimupoh quarter, but her marriage to my grandfather made her a member of the great Kabadeh quarter.

She was listed among the Kabadeh women of high repute, and her father Nyepan was a very powerful and renowned name among the Nimupoh and the entire Krahn tribe. My great grandfather Nyepan had traditional powers that he inherited from a source I cannot perfectly explain, but he specialized in treating barrenness. Barren women from far and near came to him for treatment and everyone he treated bore children. The condition was that such a woman would first bear him a child, who remained with him when she returned to her father or husband's house. This explains why the name Nyepan is such a common surname among the Sarpo.

My maternal grandfather, Tyrnyon Pantoe, was also another important personality among the Sarpos. He sat on every important matter among the six different Sarpo quarters and was known as "Wisdom House" among his peers. He was very lazy, but he had the biggest harvest every year. He was never a hunter, but always had meat in abundance. He was not a shepherd but had uncountable livestock, and he was ugly but attracted all the beautiful women. He never practiced witchcraft, but was able to reach an agreement with the entire witchcraft hierarchy in the region to determine the limits of their operation in his immediate environment. My grandfather Pantoe was also from the Kabadeh quarter and was a celebrity of sorts, even though he was not from the priesthood lineage.

The elders sent for my maternal grandfather, old man Pantoe. "We have been in search of a woman qualified to bring forth our long-awaited priest," they said. "As you know, this matter is long overdue."

Old man Pantoe nodded in agreement. Then the elders broke the news. "Your daughter Duweh was found worthy by the gods."

Old man Pantoe was happy, because this would add glory to his name. It would be recorded in Sarpo history that his grandson was a high priest, with access to the most sacred coven within the council of elders. However, it also seemed degrading to him, because my father and his daughter were closely related. This would put a stain on his reputation as a man known for wisdom.

"With all due respect, elders, how is this going to be?" Pantoe asked. "Joseph's mother is my first cousin. According to this arrangement, he would raise children through my daughter, whose bride price I have already accepted and spent. She is betrothed to another family with two children."

"We understand your fear, Wisdom House," the chief elder said, "but we do not think you have any reason to fear. Our fathers who found your daughter worthy are able to cover all reproach."

My grandfather accepted the wishes of the gods. The elders departed to call my father and disclose to him the woman the gods had chosen. When my father began to comment on the close family relationship between him and the woman, he met with the elders' stern rebuke. "Shut up! You or no one else must have any objection to whatever we say to you now. None of the elders is ready to listen to your excuse, and you dare not go against the wishes of the gods. We do not think he will accept any mistake from you this time. Now listen! Duweh is going with you to Monrovia. You shall sleep with her, and she shall give birth to a male child who will reign in your stead as our priest."

One of the elders observed that my father's passion for any other woman was relatively weak. Hence, they assigned his paternal uncle, Tweleh Falley, to cast a spell on my father so as to create a sudden burning desire for my mother. Tweleh succeeded in making my father and mother meet, and further arrangements were made to bring her to Monrovia.

When my father returned to Monrovia, his wife Ma Saybah learned she had lost her bid for her son to become the next priest, and more astonishing, that he had been utterly rejected by the gods. She became furious and determined to work out a more viable strategy. Then my father revealed that a woman had been arranged for him to sleep with in order to bring forth a male child to reign in his stead as the priest. My father assured her that as soon as the woman gave birth to a male son, the marriage will be terminated and he would live happily again with her for the rest of their lives. Obviously, Ma Saybah was not at all happy with these developments.

My mother was sent to stay with her elder sister near the Barclay Training Center (BTC) Barracks in Monrovia. Her brother-in-law, Counselor John T. Weah, planned to tell my father that she had come around. Before further arrangements were put in place, Ma Saybah consulted soothsayers who revealed that she needed to move swiftly because the woman whose child would replace her rejected son was already in town. How she found out where my mother was staying was a mystery—my father did not give her any clue. Ma Saybah's spiritualist revealed to her that my father was now a constant visitor to the barracks, so she began going there to ascertain who he was seeing there. However, she could not discover my mother, because my mother was completely protected by Nya-ghe-a-weh.

## ENDNOTE

1. Sarkpeh was one of the many chiefs from all over the country that President William V.S. Tubman brought to the city to form the first "Government of National Unity."

## Chapter 3

# THE PRIESTHOOD

According to sources, as soon as she gave birth to me, nurses surrounded my mother in astonishment. I weighed 18 pounds, a weight unsurpassed at St. Joseph Catholic Hospital in Monrovia.

Ma Saybah was brought to my mother's compound by a prophetess from the white garment denomination. They pretended to have come to congratulate the baby and his mother. The prophetess, speaking our local dialect, claimed my father was like a brother to her, and gave my mother a coin of twenty-five cents as a gift for the newborn baby. Apparently, I played with the money until my mother had need of it, but the money miraculously vanished. My mother searched the room in vain to find it. My mother consulted a soothsayer, who told her that her newborn baby was a "weird" child. The witch doctor admonished my mother to go and observe me more prudently. The man suggested that I be brought to him for further preparations. This revelation stunned my mother, but she did follow his instructions.

When all her attempts to destroy me from afar failed, Ma Saybah, still intent on regaining her son's lost priesthood, persuaded my father that I be brought home at the age of four to enjoy the privileges my brother Benedict enjoyed. While I was living in my father's house, my stepmother did everything within her power to destroy my life; but again, all her attempts failed. My stepmother, pretending she loved me, asked my father not to send me away to serve the gods of my ancestors. My stepmother often gazed at me, afraid that she was losing and sensing the premonition that an unseen, stronger power was most certainly guarding me. But at that time in my life I was oblivious of my future priesthood.

When he saw that Benedict was turning out to be a spoiled child, my father began to develop interest in me. Benedict's life deteriorated because of the curse placed on him by Nya-ghe-a-weh through the elders. My father's particular interest in me increased when Mr. Quansah, the proprietor of St. Peter's School, spoke highly of my intelligence to my father (for example, while I was in the first grade, I could solve some problems in mathematics that fourth graders could not solve). However, my father was also afraid of the threats of the elders, so he prepared my mind for the priesthood. Anytime he brought me a gift, he told me that it was from the gods of our ancestors. He also told me how highly favored I was by the gods of our ancestors.

Whenever I dreamt about blood, I had the desire to hurt some of my friends, and on occasion I did hurt them. When the reports reached my father, he would scold me in the presence of those I hurt and give them money to take care of the wounds I had afflicted. But after they left, my father would praise me for what I had done. He would also say that I was pleasing the gods of our ancestors. Sometimes at night I would have a strange urge to leave the house and sit in the market square alone. Physically I was alone, but I could feel the presence of many others around me.

## FATHER'S GAMES WITH THE GODS

My father arranged with my mother to give birth to another child, who he would eventually hand over to the village elders. Three years after the birth of the second child, Victor, the elders requested that my father send the chosen one for a formal introduction. My father sent Victor to the elders, but they rejected him, saying he was not the chosen one. They demanded that my father immediately send the one selected by the gods, because they knew he had been born. My father, being very stubborn, bluntly refused to send me to them.

After that, a sudden illness befell me, just when I was promoted to the third grade. That sickness deformed me quickly. It made me look like an ape. My looks made people call me all sorts of names, which tempted me to beat them up. My deformities did not change my father's attention for me. He took me from one native doctor to another, but they all rejected me. One particular native doctor on the Gibi Mountain rejected us after several attempts to see him. On the last attempt to see him, he nearly beat up my father because he said my spirit was overshadowing his own spirit.

After that incident, my stepmother deceitfully decided to take me to a Zoe by the name Zogboa, who won an award for being the greatest witch of her time. Zogboa was married to a man and a woman, because she was a hermaphrodite. When we arrived, the Zoe sent for my stepmother. She had learned by revelation that Ma Saybah had made several failed attempts at my life.

Zogboa told her that I was born with a destiny that could not be destroyed by any mortal being. Zogboa further stated that my stepmother had experienced strange visitations by a god because of me, and the god was greater than the god my stepmother worshiped.

For four years my father did not give up seeking a cure for me, while absolutely refusing to take me to Nya-ghe-a-weh. One day my father went to work and was visited by Nya-ghe-a-weh, whose unnatural presence filled his entire office. Everybody in the office, except my father, fell into deep sleep.

"A good-for-nothing man," Nya-ghe-a-weh said, addressing my father. "Have I not left you alone? I'm going to take my prince from your confused life and allow him to rest with his fathers. As for you and the rest of your useless father's household, you shall remain a castaway before me and those who believe in me as a great god. Furthermore, you will go mad and the things you have put before me shall be rendered useless with your own hands. The name of your father shall be cut off everywhere I command regard."

My father was trembling uncontrollably. His eyes were almost falling out of his head.

Nya-ghe-a-weh continued, "Do you think I cannot stop your so-called 'advanced life'? I could, but I knew you had made up your mind to be of no use. That was why I inspired my elders to accept your replacement."

Before my father could say a word, Nya-ghe-a-weh was gone, though my father went on to plead, "The savior of my fathers, don't go away from me. You are right! For me to ever think of fighting you was ignorance of the highest order. I acknowledge your gift of life that came to me through my forefathers. I am indeed a fool. I am a fool, I am a fool. Please come and carry your prince. There is no need to kill him. You can carry him. Oh! I was a fool..."

The cry of my father awakened his staff. "Mr. Blahyi! Mr. Blahyi!" His secretary, who helped him the first time the priestly mantle fell on him, ran to him. "What is going on, sir? You are in the office. Calm down and talk to me." He looked up, staring into the faces of his staff to see whether they had seen what he saw, but he could not tell anything from the expressions on their faces. He asked the secretary to follow him to the bathroom, and she followed him. She looked on as my father washed his face. Feeling very insecure, he asked her, "Did you or anybody see anything?"

"Like what?" the secretary asked.

"Did any of you see anything?" he screamed at the top of his voice.

Engulfed in fear, the secretary responded, "No sir, I do not understand what you are talking about. If I knew what you are asking about, I could give you a better answer."

He passed by her and declared, "It was good no one saw anything." He went back into his office, stood for a while and then directed that his office be neatly kept. He immediately closed for the day and prepared to leave.

His secretary ran after him to the office door, asking him about a document he was to sign. "I said later, Vivian!" She reluctantly went back into the office, lamenting and wondering what was going on with her boss. The behavior of my father was worrying to his immediate staff who knew him to be a quiet man. They thought he needed help, but he would not allow any of them to intervene.

## THE END OF FATHER'S GAMES

My father hurried home and took me along to Springfield, a local airport in Monrovia. We went to the house of one of my father's cousins, an aircraft engineer who lived right by Spring-field. My father greeted his wife and asked for his cousin. His wife ran and called him. When he came, my father spoke urgently. "I must leave with Milton now, Daniel. Make arrangements for one of your planes for me!"

"Kwetii,[1] what are you saying?"

"Daniel, I must go today."

"That is impossible, Joseph. Old man Zele just took the only passenger plane to Weaswa, and he won't be coming back until late at night." He asked if my father had any money on him, then left to see if he could arrange for the government six-seater air taxi.

Old man Sarkpeh, my father's uncle, came in haste. "My wife said you stopped at the house and told her you would meet me at Daniel's place. You are in a horrible mood. What's happening?"

"Oh yes, it is because of Bouye!" my father replied. (Bouye is my traditional name.)

Old man Sarkpeh could not understand when my father said it was because of me, so he asked, "What could be happening with Milton that you could not wait for me in my house and requested me to meet you at Daniel's place?"

"You don't really understand. Nya-ghe-a-weh was at my office a few hours ago. He told me Milton would die in three days time."

"Really?" old man Sarkpeh exclaimed.

"Yes," said my father. "That was why I sent for you to join me on the trip home." He then explained the rest of his experience with Nya-ghe-a-weh at his office.

Uncle Daniel came back. He announced that the plane was ready and that we had to leave at once, because the plane had to return the same day. Uncle Daniel was surprised to see Sarkpeh, so he asked him, "When did you arrive, Uncle?"

"I came in not quite long ago, Daniel," the old man replied.

"Is there anything I need to know?" Uncle Daniel asked.

"No, it is okay," my father responded, taking us to the plane.

We got to Greenville and immediately took off for Juazon, where Uncle Charlie was serving as chief messenger. We arrived in the evening. Uncle Charlie had just come from his job and was going to have his bath before supper. He was standing in front of his house with just a towel round his waist when he heard his wife and kids screaming, "Kwetii has come!"

"How are you, Aunty?" My father greeted Uncle Charlie's wife and walked toward his uncle, with Hamilton, his uncle's son, under his arm. After greeting his uncle, my father was about to bare his heart when he suddenly realized Hamilton was by his side. After sending the child away, he said, "Milton is in the car with Uncle Sarkpeh. I had an encounter with Nya-ghe-a-weh in my office today and he said he would kill Milton in three days time. If it happens, I will have been the cause of my own misfortune and destroyed what I am proud of. However, Uncle, I do not care about myself because I am guilty. But what has Milton done? He is innocent. I don't want him to die."

Uncle Charlie was speechless. "So what do you want to do?"

My father flared up in a rage. "What? You are asking me what am I going to do? I thought we were in this together. You have killed me, Charlie."

My father began to cry and ran back to the car on the road. "Sarkpeh, help me," he called. "Charlie has finished me."

Uncle Charlie was right behind him. "Wait for me, Joseph. I must come with you!"

When old man Sarkpeh asked what was going on, my father told the driver to take off and said he would explain later. "No, Joseph. Charlie is asking you to wait and you are telling us to leave? You had better pull yourself together as much as you can, because you know the people you are going to meet. Drive on," old man Sarkpeh commanded the driver.

Uncle Charlie reached the car and bent to talk to my father in the front seat. "I am sorry, Joseph. You know I will never abandon you in dangerous times like this. I am just confused."

"Don't mind him, Charlie," old man Sarkpeh interrupted, "he himself has been confused and has not been himself."

"Joseph," Charlie said, "I will come, but you must come with me to the house so that we can have a solid plan. You know what Nya-ghe-a-weh told you. He must have told the elders. They will not be on our side."

"You are right, Charlie," old man Sarkpeh said, stepping out of the car. "I have been thinking of this all along. We also need to make sure the child is prepared before handing him over to the elders. That is, if they will accept him."

"Go with Milton to the house and tell your mother to make more food," Uncle Charlie said to his son Hamilton.

## PREPARATION

I had my bath and ate so much food. Then my father, Uncle Charlie, old man Sarkpeh, and Uncle Tweleh took me into a little hut in front of the house. My father began to ask me if I knew who Nya-ghe-a-weh was. "Yes. Is he not the one that sent me lots of gifts when I was much younger?"

"Yes, my son, you have not forgotten," my father held my head in his chest, stroking my hair.

"Are we going to see him?" I asked.

"Yes," said Uncle Charlie, looking into my face. "Would you like to see him?"

"Yes, Uncle, I am ready. Let's go."

"Right, Milton. Don't be in a hurry. He has always loved and yearned to see you, but what will you do if he does not allow you to return with us?"

"I will stay with him, as long as it won't be a problem to my father. My father loves me too."

My father whispered across my head in a weeping tone, "Yes, Milton, I love you. I love my son. But..."

I looked into my father's face and said, "Don't cry, Papa." In my innocence and ignorance I told my father not to struggle over the decision to leave me behind. "I will pretend before Nya-ghe-a-weh that I'll be seeing you off."

"No, Milton, you can stay with him if he asks you to do so," my father said.

By that point, my father could not hold back his tears. He left me and went behind the house. Uncle Charlie kept me from following my father. "Let us wait for the old man. He went to see if Nya-ghe-a-weh is ready to see you, after which he will hand you over to him. Your father is just considering your absence back home, but he really wants you to be with Nya-ghe-a-weh. He will make you a powerful warrior."

"Did you say a warrior?"

"Yes."

"Like Vic Morrow in 'Combat'?"

"You got it right, Milton."

"Are you sure he can make me like Vic Morrow?"

"I am very sure! You are going to be more than Vic Morrow."

All of a sudden, we began to hear shouts of jubilation all over the place.

"What is going on?" old man Sarkpeh asked, coming out of the hut.

"Monrovia has really made you people strangers," someone said. "Why don't you go up town if you want to hear the news."

"What do you mean, brother?"

"The resounding noise you are hearing is that of the bell of the elders' town crier, so you will certainly find out what the matter is."

"Yes, I know this. But what I am hearing does not sound like a bell."

Just as they were arguing with each other, the messenger came near, announcing the good news that the long-awaited priest had arrived and the ceremony to usher the priest into office would begin on the following day. The messenger said, "Do take note, only males are to be seen. Men are charged to help women in chores that demand their coming out of the house. These restrictions also affect those men whom by the standard of this community are not worth being called a man. In strict compliance to our culture, youths are to help rebuild old thatches. Men are to gather at the town square by midday tomorrow, and are expected to stay in the square until the ceremony is completely over. The elders want you to know that this enthronement ceremony is long overdue. The last one was sixty-one years ago. They know your so-called modern life has the tendency to devalue the traditional practices of the forefathers. Therefore, you are warned to govern yourself and observe all that you are told."

My uncles were not sure whether the announcement was referring to me, seeing as nobody knew I had been brought as demanded. After thinking about it, however, Tweleh and my uncle realized the gods might have known I was around. While they were discussing this possibility, the driver who brought us attempted to start the vehicle's engine, but it would not start. It became obvious that there was no going back. All activity had been prohibited that day and throughout the night.

At midnight, Nya-ghe-a-weh appeared to my father while he was fast asleep and said, "Why are you so stubborn? Do you know I can choose to stop you from ever returning to Monrovia?"

"Yes, I know you can," my father answered, shivering.

"I don't like seeing you this way. Don't be afraid of me. You have erred by thinking you could play the fool, but you are my priest. Bouye is just a replacement. The only thing you don't know is that I don't ever turn down requests from my priest. This is the reason I consented to your appeal for your son to reign in your stead. Your appeal for a replacement was the first of its kind. It is also standard that only first male children are selected as priests. Moreover, nobody below forty has ever become priest. But the love I have for you and the tribe constrained me. Honestly, I forgive you. My masquerade bearer and the warriors are behind the house. Wake up the lad and tell him I have sent for him."

"You are truly worthy of the fathers' worship. Thank you very much. I will do just as you wish."

My father tried waking up Uncle Charlie, but couldn't. Then he came to me and told me what had transpired between him and Nya-ghe-a-weh at midnight. He explained the messenger's announcement, and told me Nya-ghe-a-weh would be sending his warriors to me.

I was excited. "Did you say warriors? Do they have guns? Where are they?"

"No, son. Don't be afraid. Why would they come with guns? They did not come to harm you."

"I am not afraid, Dad! I want to get to him quickly so that he will make me a warrior like Vic Morrow."

My father was surprised. He had not heard Uncle Charlie and me discussing Vic Morrow.

# INITIATION

I will never forget the moment my father handed me over to the tribe's warriors. I expected to see them in army uniforms with guns in their hands. Instead, muscular, naked men with spears and daggers in their hands saluted me. I was not afraid from the beginning. Even while they led me through the thick forests, I tried to be friendly. I asked them some questions and tried to interact, but they were absolutely mute, as the culture demands that the priest be treated with due respect. The only sounds I could hear from them were woofing, barking, and groaning noises from their closed mouths. The shouting of Nya-ghe-a-weh's masquerade was behind us.[2]

The warriors carried me, and the group of Nya-ghe-a-weh masquerade bearers passed us. The warriors stopped and chanted war songs round about me till the council of elders got to where we were. They left me behind with the elders, who bathed me. The elders soon told me that Nya-ghe-a-weh had been waiting for me. I came to my senses and became inquisitive. They responded to my numerous questions, and I became more relieved. Before the break of dawn, the elders quickly put me into their court, situated in the town square. They decked me with a piece of leather around my waist to cover my private parts, and pieces of leather on my left arm and right wrist. Then they hung a leather bag containing chalk on my shoulders. From the time I entered the town, they began to drum persistently. The drumming continued until the ordination ceremony was over.

By noon, the town square was crowded with men and a few women. When I stepped out of the elder's court into the midst of the people, their accolades went to my head. The elders were in a terrible dither about putting a rope on me. They had made a resolution that they would tie a rope on anyone who said he had encountered Nya-ghe-a-weh and was chosen as the next priest, for many people had lied and were then struck dead by Nya-ghe-a-weh. In the end, I entered the sacred fenced court of Nya-ghe-a-weh without a rope tied around me.

The elders stopped before the gate, reciting enchantments to the silenced fathers in different tones and voices. "Fathers of old, fathers of old." As I entered the thick and heavy presence of Nya-ghe-a-weh, I could barely walk upright, and I could no longer communicate with the elders. My eyes became dim and everything around me became blurry. I could not see anything. After some time, my ears opened to the spirit world, and I heard strange laughter. Then, a domineering voice directed me to lick the chalk in the bag for strength. I kept licking the chalk, as I needed it for the journey.

The distance between the rock and where I had left the elders was only about two hundred and fifty meters, but the atmosphere was so heavy that I could only progress very slowly. I got to the big rock, Nya-ghe-a-weh's throne, at night. I stood before the big rock for three days and nights, depending on the chalk for food. I was also sustained by the unceasing praises showered on me by a mysterious voice.

At midnight of the third day, the rock tilted upward, and something like a stool came out from beneath the rock. A strange, audible voice directed me to stand on the stool. After I complied with the order, the weird stool began to descend beneath the rock, and the part of the rock that had tilted upward to admit me gradually returned to its normal position. While I was being carried into the rock, everything around me became dark and darker until it was completely dark. But when everything stopped moving, I could see as far as my eyes could view.

## DE-PROGRAMMED AND PROGRAMMED

I was bewildered when it became possible for me to see again. Suddenly, I saw Nya-ghe-a-weh quickly dragging its feet toward me. He was a gigantic figure, about twelve feet high and wearing old rags that looked as if they were just taken from the mud. He had bruises all over his left side, and his left wing was folded under his arm, making his hand stuck to his chest. He moved his right leg twice, then dragged his left leg to catch up. He had a very big rod in his hand. Despite his disabilities he moved fast. "My son, you are welcome."

As he came closer to me, I asked him, "Are you Nya-ghe-a-weh? I want be a warrior."

He laughed. "You are a warrior already, though your father wasted your time. But not to worry, you are never late."

I did not see anything that looked like light under the rock, but somehow I could see as far as I looked. I was walking by the right side of Nya-ghe-a-weh. With his hand on my shoulder, he pointed at what looked like a screen, and directed me to look at it. On the screen I saw my mother with a baby on her lap. He asked me, "Can you identify who they are?

I replied, "Yes! The woman is my mother, but I do not know who the baby is."

"Ha, ha!" Nya-ghe-a-weh laughed, "That was you when you were a baby."

"Really?" I exclaimed.

"Certainly," he replied. Then he asked me if I knew the next person on the screen.

"Yes! She is Ma Saybah, my stepmother." She was half dressed with some black powder in her hand, which she took from a calabash on the ground. An old lady had given the calabash to her. She blew the dust and recited incantations. I did not hear any voice, but could tell she was speaking. I saw the powder sail through the air till it got to my mother and me. However, before the powder diffused on us, I saw a wide shadow spread over my mother and me.

That first day, I saw scenes from the first year of my life displayed on the screen. The second day, I watched scenes from my second year, and on the third day from my third year. Each scene revealed the wide shadow spread over my mother and me whenever there was any attempt to harm us.

Nya-ghe-a-weh expatiated eloquently on the scenes from the screen, deliberately showing me the dangers I was protected from by the shadow. Nya-ghe-a-weh's persistent and strong emphasis on the shadow motivated me to inquire from him whose shadow it was. In response, he urged me to turn to him. He stepped aside to allow me see the reflection of his shadow. When I obliged, I exclaimed, "It is your shadow!"

"Yes, I have been the one protecting you all along, because you are my Hero. (This is what he called me until things felt apart.) You shall be the greatest in your time and admired by all. No human being can stand up to you or equal the status you shall attain as my priest. Men shall hold you in high regard."

On the seventh day, he showed me how the same shadow stood over me for some time and would signal me to follow it. The shadow led me at midnight to the marketplace and other isolated places. I also saw the shadow standing over me in class while I was still in school.

The screening of my seventh year revealed Ma Saybah accompanying an old lady who came to our house for a few days. The old lady drew my attention when I saw her hand over to Ma Saybah a fan she was holding. She urged her to fan me while I was fast asleep. After that, she washed her private parts and poured the water on my face. Then Ma Saybah went straight into the house, while the woman departed to Teleweyan's house immediately. Interestingly, while Ma Saybah and her cohort where executing their evil act, I did not notice the wide shadow around me. It became obvious that this was how I contracted the sickness that deformed me.

I demanded to know why the shadow didn't show up. Nya-ghe-a-weh responded thus: "I thought that it would make your father swiftly refer you to me, as I thought it would be a mystery to him. But he stuck to his guns. Moreover, he preferred your stepmother's counsel and went to seek solution in the hands of those who are not even your equals."

On the eighth day, he showed me on the screen the places where my father took me, and how he went ahead to warn the witch doctors to refer my father to him. He was smart to let me see the way he devastated those witch doctors who did not heed his warnings with a wave of the hand. I asked him why he didn't allow other people to treat me if he claimed to love me. In his deceit, he told me that other forces were aware that I would be great, and thus they wanted to take me captive to deprive him of my person.

On the ninth, tenth, and eleventh days, I saw elaborate scenes of the history of the entire tribe from the point he met the tribe through the most recent battles. He referred to the Sarpo founding father that left his fathers' land for Greenville as a coward. I also saw priests and other elders he described as being loyal to him. "These men were steadfast and dedicated to me in their time," he assured me. He did not show me other ancient fathers like Nnawyilee, his father, and my grandfather old man Blahyi.

In my heart I was furious. I did not see why their good intentions should by ignored by Nya-ghe-a-weh. Some of the people Nya-ghe-a-weh referred to as "useless" were destroyed by him. He hypnotized them into eating things that were taboos like kola nuts, or he would bring them in contact with the priest, after which Nya-ghe-a-weh would kill them on the grounds that they had been unfaithful.

After seeing those powerful things and people, I yearned dearly to be very powerful and great. In my doggedness, I was full of myself. I then turned to Nya-ghe-a-weh and said, "I will not be unfaithful to you like those who allowed women to stand between you and them."

"In fact," he replied, "you shall remain very special to me, and I will make you greater than other men in your time."

"Great one, I will not lose such powers. I shall follow all your instructions...if I could see myself turn into a lion, tiger, and eagle."

The old trickster laughed as if he was already winning. "Did I hear you say 'turn into a lion, tiger, and eagle?'" He was trying to come down to my level. He put his face in my face, pulled me to himself with his right hand, stuffed me under his left broken wing and flew all over the place in excitement, saying, "Lion, tiger, eagle, elephant, bush cow, wolves, and everything in the forest you could turn into. But they are all child's play to what I want you to be in your time."

## INITIATION RITES AND EMPOWERMENT

On the eleventh and final day of my initiation, Nya-ghe-a-weh put me on a huge, sharp piece of rock and disappeared. Suddenly,

I saw a calabash gourd beneath the rock containing flesh soaked in fresh blood. I then heard his voice from afar echoing in my ears, "Get down and take your lonely meal."

There was no way for me to climb down that sharp rock. But just before I could say, "I cannot," I heard him say, "Don't ever say you can't, because you are a hero. You can do anything you wish to do, especially if I asked you to do so." Immediately, a strange courage engulfed me. I swiftly changed my sitting position, squatted, and then flew down the rock, shrieking like a warrior. As I landed on the ground, the praises of the fathers started again. I started running on my heels from one side to another and flapping my arms like a bird intending to fly. I got to the calabash and sat down with my legs around it. I dipped my hands into it, lifted the flesh and started to eat. I was very hungry. When I finished eating the lonely meal, I stood up and continued the war dance in response to the praises of the fathers from the land of the dead around the piece of rock.

Then Nya-ghe-a-weh appeared behind me. He passed me and walked toward the rock, signaling for me to follow him. After we stood before the rock for some time, he turned to me and told me to enter into it even though it was without an opening. I moved toward the rock, and it began to open. As I entered the rock, Nya-ghe-a-weh was satisfied, and he repeated these few words, "I will make you my greatest priest ever."

In the rock were two stools shaped alike. The bigger one was about ten feet in height, and the smaller one was almost two feet. On top of the small stool was a special knife, well carved with black stones engraved on the handle. By the knife was a talisman that looked like the tail of an animal engraved with cowry shells on the handle. There were also eleven other cowry shells of different sizes on the smaller stool. The rock was narrow, without space to twist or turn around. Nya-ghe-a-weh sat on the bigger stool while I stood before him.

"You need to understand how you can maintain the powers and responsibilities I am about to put in your care. First, I want you to know that whatever transpires between you and me is highly confidential. If you reveal what transpires between you and me to others, you will expose the source of your powers. Be informed that these powers belong to you and the entire tribe before and after you. Any act of treason shall result in death.

"You will not eat or have anything to do with kola nuts. Touching, not to mention eating, kola nuts is tantamount to playing with the covenant I made with the tribe, because kola nuts were the bane of that covenant.

"Since you are very young for the power you are about to use, you must make human sacrifices on a monthly basis at the appearing of the new moon. These will enable you retain the powers you received. Failure or delay from your quarters shall result in your demise. Your office will be given to another."

Nya-ghe-a-weh then instructed me to swallow each of the cowry shells, which eventually entered into parts of my body. The cowry shells served as remote controls to eleven different powers he gave me. The three in my left hand were for the two kinds of disappearance and reappearance. The two in my right hand would contact the supernatural knife and the stool of authority. Two in my left thigh were for protection from bullets and knives. In my right thigh, the cowry shell were used to hypnotize and invoke the spirits of fear on people or prey that came my way. The last two were somewhere in my system, though I could not pinpoint their position, and I did not have control over them. One was to monitor me and the other was to stir up anger in me against things that Nya-ghe-a-weh did not like.

He instructed me to stretch forth my hands and touch the cowry shell that was in my right hand. A knife suddenly appeared in my hand. Then I was asked to sit on the stool and touch the second shell in my right hand. The stool started to fly, and took me straight into the midst of my ancestors. They were about two hundred or more in number, all sitting around a very wide woods with their legs folded under them. They had a clay plate with powder-like chalk on it, which was described as the food of our great ancestors. From the looks on their faces they cheerfully received me.

Nya-ghe-a-weh instructed the ancestors, "Go ahead and tell him things you intended to achieve in your days that you fell short of because of time." One after the other, they came from the woods, walking through the right flank of Nya-ghe-a-weh. They each related the services they were unable to render during their reign as priest. Nya-ghe-a-weh challenged me to achieve those things my predecessors could not achieve. Thereafter, I appealed to Nya-ghe-a-weh to support me in realizing this great task. I reflected on the numerous powers he gave me, and felt nothing could stop me from achieving the elders' requests.

Suddenly Nya-ghe-a-weh's laws and the accompanying death penalty came to my mind in relation to the elders he described as failures. Though they did not eat or touch kola nuts literally, they were contaminated by a third party. I then asked, "How can I discern someone who may have eaten or played with kola nuts before reaching me?" None of the elders could look Nya-ghe-a-weh directly in his face. They were guilt-stricken as they looked at each other. Nya-ghe-a-weh looked at them for conspiratorial cover-up. My question was like a bombshell in their midst. They were all caught unaware because they expected me to be naïve, being the youngest priest ever enthroned. They were all astonished, including Nya-ghe-a-weh, because I was the only one who ever questioned Nya-ghe-a-weh.

After a prolonged silence, he asked me to follow him. Carried by the stool, we went back into the huge rock. Reluctantly, he said, "I will give you a spirit that will detect anyone who ate a kola nut." Finally he warned me to stay away from the masquerade, except when occasion warranted it. My ears were opened to the dancing and singing outside. I started to dance with the magical knife and the talisman in my hands. I came out of the huge rock dancing as the rock that covered us began to lift off. The ray of light penetrated through the opening, and the very stool appeared that had first brought me. I stood on it and it carried me back to the surface.

## BUILDING A NEW PRIESTLY ORDER

I shrieked as soon as I surfaced from beneath the rock. Immediately, the elders announced my return. Nya-ghe-a-weh's masquerade chased back into their houses the women and other people who do not belong to the masquerade caucus.

I then entered the elders' hut and gave them instructions on things I wanted. I met with old man Jay Swen for proper briefing and handing over of matters pertaining to the tribe. On handing over to me, it became clear that most of old man Jay Swen's rulings were based on personal gain. I lifted the embargo he had placed on the people, including the witches he stopped from operating. However, I issued a stern warning to limit their functions until I put things in proper order.

I spent another six or seven days with the elders while waiting for my father to take me back to Monrovia. My father came and paid me due respect as his priest. Nya-ghe-a-weh had warned me that since I had requested to be with my father in Monrovia, I should live as any other child, though it was also resolved that I would make necessary provisions for Nya-ghe-a-weh's daily visit. This was necessary, as I needed to be quickly acquainted with issues pertaining to the priesthood.

I got to my father's house in Monrovia and began to work out a suitable atmosphere in the vicinity in strict compliance to Nya-ghe-a-weh's orders. After all the ceremonies to accommodate Nya-ghe-a-weh's visitation were completed, he began to visit as we had discussed. His visits took place between midnight and four in the morning. We took soul trips via abstract planes[3] to people who used his powers to receive dues. In order to secure the atmosphere (spiritual realm) from other forces interfering to our free flow, I took on a campaign to banish all the surrounding witch doctors. I started with old man Morlu (a native doctor), Ma Porteah-dee (a white garment prophetess who usually accompanied my stepmother), and Ma Saybah herself, whom I spiritually impregnated for life.

Initially, my monthly human sacrifice was taken from Kota-ti's yard, where I was brought up. However, my conscience was greatly troubled after each sacrifice when I heard the victims' parents weep for their loved ones. I decided to go far away to find my prey. At twelve years old, I became known all over Monrovia and its suburbs for playing draughts (checkers). I went from community to community in pretence to play, but my objective was to get used to the names and the spiritual countenance of their faces. Knowing the name of a person and his or her spiritual countenance gave me easier access to them in the dream or spirit world. However, if I did not succeed in securing a far-away victim on time, I resorted to offering any of the close residents.

I will quickly enlighten you on what I choose to call "spiritual countenance." The phrase implies an instinct that captures a person's spiritual expression by which he or she can be easily identified in the spirit realm. If you come across somebody in the spirit realm, you cannot easily identify the person if you don't understand the spiritual countenance dimension, even though you knew him or her very well in the physical. Spiritual countenance is easily ascertained when somebody is meditating, frightened, happy, or sad. These exercises pave the way for the human spirit to come out of the being. Spiritualists capitalize on any of these actions to mark or identify their targets when they summon human spirits in time of need. Nothing exposes spiritual countenance as meditation, fright, happiness, and sadness. They are all products of the spirit.

Another vital access to identify a person in the spirit world is his or her name. I took time to learn people's names in readiness for the sacrifice. In steady effort I waited till whomever I had decided to target for sacrifice was asleep. Only when somebody is asleep can the person succumb to spiritual calls, because the human spirit departs from the body when human beings are asleep. To the best of my knowledge, there are three genres of spiritual windows that the human spirit can go to during sleep— land, forest, and air. Whenever I conjured the spirit of my target, I did so through any of those windows.

Maybe this explanation will help you understand my point. If you are looking for someone called J.D., and you find yourself standing before a hall with several people with that name, all those people will respond when you say their name. You should be able to identify the J.D. you are looking for. In the realm of the spirit, your ability to identify the particular person depends on the spiritual description at your disposal. This is the usual process I used in offering sacrifices. Once the person was asleep, I went to any of the windows, summoned the spirit, and bound and dedicated it to Nya-ghe-a-weh. He held back the person's spirit and prevented it from returning to the body. A human being is certified clinically dead, despite all scientific measures, when the spirit does not return to the human body. After the person is confirmed dead and buried, we then programmed the spirit for evil. Such spirits are responsible for strange movements in houses.

## MAMMY

I came into contact with a little girl called Mammy and decided to use her for sacrifice to Nya-ghe-a-weh. I invoked her spirit three times, but she miraculously escaped. I had never encountered this in my dealing with Nya-ghe-a-weh. I decided to use another victim for the sacrifice, as my deadline was fast approaching. He refused the sacrifice and told me to bring that particular girl. I told him how I had tried but was not successful. He told me to give her a gift that would be used as a medium for legal entry into her life. This I did, but the girl refused it, because her mother and her Sunday school teacher cautioned her not to accept gifts from strangers. My inability to have easy access to Mammy's life was due to the fact that her mother always took her to church.

I went to Nya-ghe-a-weh and appealed for a substitute, with a promise that I would make Mammy available in my next sacrifice. Nya-ghe-a-weh became furious over my appeal. "If you should remain the first and greatest among the priest of the past, in your time and the future, you dare not settle for failure and crave for another option!" He then devised another strategy, which was to give the girl's mother a gift. I took twenty-five cents as a form of dowry for Mammy. Seeing me as a child, she accepted it and told her friends what I had said to her. They began to laugh at me and said, "As young as he is, he wants a woman and went as far as paying a dowry? You can accept the money."

Just about that time the little girl entered the house carrying water on her head. Jokingly, her mother said, "Mammy, this is your husband. He just paid your dowry."

I then left because my mission was accomplished. I entered my coven that night and invoked her spirit. She appeared and wanted to escape. I then told her that she could not go since she had now become legally mine by virtue of her mother's decision. The next morning, Mammy was discovered dead.

Another time, a particular local clan chief with thirteen children came to seek my aid in leading his people. I accepted and assured him of my support. However, I told him to bring a fowl to facilitate the work. Without any delay, he brought the fowl and my work started in earnest. I held the fowl and circled it around his head. Then I asked him to imagine the person he loved best in his life.

"What for?" he asked.

I said, "So that the same love you have for that person will spill into the villagers' to love you and be willing to do anything for you."

He consented and asked me to continue. I began to circle the fowl around his head. When I saw it done, I stopped and asked him to strike the fowl on the head with a dried, tiny straw. He obeyed, and instantly the fowl died, but the face of his only daughter appeared as he looked at the fowl's face. "What have you done?" he asked, positioning himself to raise an alarm.

"You dare not yell."

Shivering, he said, "I hope you have not killed my only daughter."

"That was exactly what you saw. Be a man. As you know, nothing goes for nothing. Hold your tongue in this matter, or else I'll finish you," I warned him.

When he approached his house from the forest, the thunderous weeping of his wife, children, and other mourners pierced him like a nail. He yelled, "What happened to my only daughter?"

The girl had asked to join her brothers and mother to pound rice. Not wanting to hurt her feelings, they obliged her, as she was loved much by everybody in her family. As she began to pound the rice, she slipped off the stool she stood on and the pestle hit the back of her neck. She died instantly.

Seeing the chief's uncontrollable state, I feared that he might not be able to hold back the true cause of the accident. Therefore, I struck him with the spirit of madness. Everyone felt that he had something to do with the death of his daughter because of his instant madness after her death.

## HOW I ENLARGED NYA-GHE-A-WEH'S COAST

I started "blind witch recruitments" by going to wells where communities get their drinkable water. I planted charms in them so that anyone who drank the water from the wells would become a medium to display my craft.

As a tribal priest, I did everything to see the elevation of my tribal men when they solicited me for what they lacked the power to accomplish. Whenever they made their intention known to me, my service mandate demanded that I provide the means for them to accomplish their heart's desires. I would simply look through the levels and evaluate the task against their power. If the task was attainable using their remaining power, we gave them the so-called grace and blessing from the gods.

I believe that every man is given a measure of power to fulfill his God-given purpose on earth. Every measure of power lasts for a given period. If a man is destined to be a millionaire at age forty, God gave him the ability to understand the process by which this destiny can be fulfilled. Well, if such a person is a member of my tribe and wishes to become a millionaire before the ordained time, I would program his abilities to match his request by stealing power from others. Unfortunately, if he is not prudent enough, he will end up broke for the rest of his life. This is the reason many who attained instant wealth suddenly become poor without hope in sight, and die without a trace that they were ever wealthy.

This explains the reason no Julukon man, despite his pomp and elegance while he was alive, ever left inheritance for his offspring. My uncle, Lawrence Fallah, a son of my father's Aunt Portea, traveled almost all over the world when he was controlling a logging company, but died without a chicken or trace of money. Another late uncle discovered a gold deposit worth more than $20 million. He was also privileged to travel almost all over the world, but after his death, there was nothing. My father was the chief accountant in the Ministry of Finance. He also gained money left by Steven Tolbert before he met his untimely death. Today, there is no trace of my late father's wealth.

The only way I could given my tribesmen power was by stealing it from another person. Most members of my tribe operate on a zero-balance virtue level, because when Nya-ghe-a-weh made his foolish covenant with the tribe through old man Saydee, he imposed that the tribe and everything about them belonged to him. So I stole other people's powers to make up for the poor power level of my tribesmen, and to prove my priestly role. This is why I went into blind-witch recruitment—for a higher power network.

For my recruitment, I would usually tie ropes around a lot of coins on which I had cast a spell. To get my prospective customers to buy my charms, I played on their intelligence by flattering them that the charms possessed the power to enable a child to walk early and cure deadly childhood diseases. The values I placed on my charms attracted many parents who would tie them round their children's waists according to my prescription. My ulterior motive was to gain easier access to the entire vicinity where any child wearing my talisman resided. The ropes around the coins turned into to snakes at night and drained the blood of other children in the area.

I was able to establish four hundred covens for Nya-ghe-a-weh in and outside Liberia. Only seventy-one of such covens did not have altars.

A coven is the congregation of priests that owe allegiance to a god, before whom they come together once in a while to receive instructions and appraisal. However, a priest compulsorily attends to an altar, as an altar represents the manifold presence of the god. A coven without an altar is like the Tabernacle of old without the Ark of the Covenant. Every altar built by the people of Israel signifies God's presence, with the conviction that God actually dwelt in the altar. (God even reminded Jacob to remember his promise of building Him an altar in a particular spot if He brought him back to it again.)

Whenever I set up a coven for a witch doctor or anybody of similar rank, their ability to display power as I did would elevate them to be a priest, and I would build an altar in the coven they controlled. If the priest was committed and crafty enough, the number of people he manipulated would grow rapidly. I was not able to monitor all of these priests personally; I was like a general overseer. Monitoring and paying special attention to a local coven would have been a waste of time. Rather, I planted altars representing Nya-ghe-a-weh, and my priests all registered their respective victims on the altars, which enabled us to monitor them closely. The special endowment to register his victims and communicate with us (Nya-ghe-a-weh and me) through that altar qualified him to be a priest.

A witch doctor or wizard pretends that his main job is to solve problems in a village, town, or community. In most cases, his curses and spells are the cause of the problems he then cures. However, his real mission in these exchanges is to plant a lifeline between his god and the victim, which gives the victim and the god equal access to each other. Of course, the god knows his way to the victim, but the victim might not know until he is initiated into the craft.

Again, without access to man, a demonic spirit remains powerless. Though God Almighty is the sole owner and Creator of earth, He has given the earth to man that they may take charge over it. Earth is reserved for the exploits of man, not spirits. When a spirit has access to man, however, it can legally function on earth. When a witch doctor gives the god access to a victim, the god can accomplish things through the victim.

The apostle Paul said, "...it is no longer I who live, but Christ lives in me..." (Gal. 2:20). Paul said this because his education did not give him the extra abilities Christ gave him. Christ's access to him accomplished what the Adamic nature had limited in man. A demonic spirit might not be able to work all things as Christ did through Paul, but it will work many things through the person it has access to. As Christ claims and protects you if you have accepted Him, so a spirit claims and protects the one who accepts him.

If a so-called witch doctor succeeds in bringing a good percentage of the people in his area under his god, other spiritualists will submit to his claim and will not try to hunt those people. They cannot hunt a person carrying a god's mark without consulting the god. If he is crafty enough, a witch doctor will bring other spiritualists and their followers under his control. As his influence expands, his power increases and he may not even ask for an altar when we give it to him.

As I came to know later, God Almighty, the Father of my Savior Jesus Christ, is greater than any spirit, coven, evil altar, or false god, as it says in First John 4:4, "You are of God, little children, and have overcome them, because *He who is in you is greater than he who is in the world.*"

## ENDNOTES

1. Kwetii is my father's traditional name.

2. Masquerades, which exist in many of the tribal societies throughout West Africa, portray the true images of tribal gods. They are a modified form of worship linking humans to an idol. Gods (demonic powers) can only manifest their stolen powers through men or animals. Humans without personal control are vulnerable to them, particularly to the god's offer of unusual abilities. After a god establishes rapport with its human counterpart, it directs the person

to make an idol representing the god's identity. Every man, woman, boy, or girl who affiliates with such an idol in any way consciously or unconsciously becomes accessible to the god.

A god called Bog first introduced masquerade in the Ethiopian empire. His priest is called "Bogus," meaning "Bog's carrier." But powerful spirits like Nya-ghe-a-weh, Havieso (a god of lightning who controls Togo and Benin Republic), and Sakahmonue (a god from the sea responsible to coastal Ghana) see masquerade as being for weaker gods. I came in contact with Bog on two occasions, when he came to collect his homage. Every god that uses a masquerade pays homage to Bog, but he complained to me that the three gods named here do not bring his homage to him. When he came to collect it by himself, Bog was derided by his colleague Nya-ghe-a-weh. That was how I got to know that supergods do not take delight in the masquerades.

The masquerade for Nya-ghe-a-weh was established by the priest before me, who felt it would help the people embrace the fellowship of Nya-ghe-a-weh and show their honor and love for him, since direct access to the god is limited to the priests. Non-insiders think the masquerade as Nya-ghe-a-weh itself. Men and women who do not hold strong membership, and all children except first sons, do not see even the masquerade.

3. Astral projection.

## Chapter 4

# THE PRIEST BECOMES GENERAL BUTT NAKED

The late president of Liberia, Samuel K. Doe (1951-1990), was a member of the Krahn tribe, so he was automatically placed under my jurisdiction as the priest of the biggest god from the Krahn tribe. I promised him my full support if he would be enlisted among my priests. He accepted, and became the seventh in rank among the 3,929 priests under my control. Remember, one must have an altar in his coven before becoming a priest, and to have an altar, you need many people under you. Almost all of Doe's cabinet and other strategic officials from his time in power were initiated and dedicated to Nya-ghe-a-weh from the president's executive coven.

We also asked the late president to bring the nation under the control of Nya-ghe-a-weh so that the presidency would be limited to the Krahn tribe, just as his priesthood is limited to the Julukon. We asked him to officially turn the nation over to us by giving up the flag and the seal of the Republic of Liberia. He did so, and we ritually assigned them to the lineage of the Krahn tribe and had them planted in the Gedeh Mountain, which is the powerhouse of our tribe. We also programmed Liberia to reject any leadership not from the Krahn tribe, thereby giving Nya-ghe-a-weh direct access and complete control over the government.

I also placed Nya-ghe-a-weh among the first three high-ranking deities in the West Africa's black witch coastline division. The witchcraft of West Africa is divided into three major dimensions, black witch, red witch, and white witch, and each of them operates by divisions. The black witch, which I understood well, is divided into three divisions, the coastline, the land, and the forest divisions. The coastline division is comprised of the gods found along the coastlines. I took over the headship of the coastline division from a priest in Ghana. He had held the position for many years and refused to turn over the post to me on grounds that I was a youngster and would be unable to control such an organization with more than two hundred thousand gods and their priests.

However, though I was young, my incomparable achievements in a very short while qualified me to take over the post. I used the office of the late president to promote our southeastern craft, and to silence two major crafts in the nation, the Masonic and the Poro and Sande crafts. The Gios' control over the government permitted me to have national influence as a key player.

I gave all my support to the late President Samuel K. Doe in the 1985 parliamentary and presidential elections in return for his loyalty to me. I manipulated almost the whole nation to vote for him. I planted blind agents in all major restaurants and bakeries to sell his fame. I extracted white blood cells from persons

I felt qualified for the ritual, invoked the fame of the president into them, and distributed them in small capsules. I gave them to the blind agents and instructed them to put them in all the food and bread they prepared. We automatically controlled any-one who ate any of those specially prepared meals, which is how they were led to vote for him.

The same human oil was taken to big gatherings of opposition parties and placed in their refreshments. As they consumed the food, they became accessible to us. We monitored them, knew their plans, and placed confusion among them. For example, we called one of the opposition members and told him that a col-league of his was speaking against the president. We stated his exact suggestions as if he had actually said it. When the person listening unwittingly accused their colleague to the president, the president took retribution from there. Along with my priest-hood, I had a gang that I used for stealing weapons.

## MY PRIESTLY ROLE

My priestly role became more crucial when Charles Ghankay Taylor led the National Patriotic Front of Liberia (NPFL) to war against my tribe. The battle had three main arms: propaganda, "barrel of the gun," and spiritual. The propaganda mechanism provoked the Krahn tribe into a state of confusion, causing the tribe to show the nation its worst. The propaganda was so effec-tive and sweeping that other Kwa-speaking groups sharing the same culture and language with the Krahn were killed or forced to flee the country. Some of them joined forces with the NPFL until our people were pushed to the wall, leaving us no alterna-tive but to hold together and fight back.

The "barrel of the gun" arm of the war was strategically placed in the hands of men from two of the bravest and strongest tribes who already considered Krahn enemies. It is even recorded in the early history of the nation that these two warring tribes, the Gio and Manu, fought together against the Krahn in a series of battles. These two tribes are from Nimba County and share common boundaries with the Krahn in Grand Gedeh County.

When the People's Redemption Council (PRC), led by Samuel K. Doe, originally came to power, the dispute between the Grand Gedein and Nimbanain was expected to come to an end because two of the strongest members controlling the helm of state power and security came from those tribes. Chairman Master Sergeant Samuel K. Doe was from Grand Gedeh County, and Thomas Quiwonkpa, the Commanding General of the Liberian Armed Forces, was from Nimba County. They started the settlement process, but it came to an end when Doe appointed Quiwonkpa as the Secretary General of the then-ruling military council. This did not go down well with the General, so he refused the appointment.

The spiritual arm of the war erected other demonic powers in the nation that had at first been crushed by President Doe through our tribal influence, because he was one of us. Besides the re-erection of other local powers, Charles Taylor brought other powerful priests with him from Mali, Burkina Faso, and other places.

The NPFL war against the PRC and the Krahn tribe was strategic and successful to some extent. The strategies left the tribe very unpopular, to the point that we could hardly attract any sympathy from the other tribes in the nation. The name Krahn became an abomination. The sons and daughters of the tribe did not want to be identified with us, because a household could be exterminated if a single Krahn man was found in the midst.

The feelings of rejection brought out the true warring nature in the tribe. In time of war, the service of the priest is essential to the tribe. President Doe sent for other traditional rulers, including: old man Jay Swen, Nyenplu Taylor, and Juezeo Barway (both traditional warriors, leaders, and hunters); old man Tarnue, a Zoe from Lofa County; old man Ghee, a Zoe from Margibi County; and many others from different parts of the country. The first three traditional leaders and myself formed the inner caucus. We were the most trusted because we came from the same region. We asked the other traditional leaders from the other regions to operate by themselves in order to avoid a mixture of powers (though actually, we were just being selfish).

Old man Jay Swen and I were the only active priests in this group. However, old man Swen used his long experience in the realms of the spirit to see that the battle would eventually turn against us. Swen left the presidential mansion, promising to bring down his masquerade from his village, but we later discovered that he had defected from our camp and was consulting for Charles Taylor. His betrayal was not that surprising to us, because he was already known as a commercial, inconsistent, and selfish priest. He used tribal power for financial gain and to empower his children. His son, J. Apollo Swen Jr., set one of the unusual fighting records in the crisis by the power his father gave him. Swen Jr. fought for the government and displayed the same inconsistency as his father by fighting for several warring factions, including Mr. Taylor.

Old man Swen was powerful and experienced in playing the craft, but was no threat to us until he started revealing our secret codes of access to our spheres of spiritual power and authority, though he did not use them by himself because he knew the risk involved. Almost all the people that used our codes did not return untouched; in fact, many were killed. As a result of his betrayal, we had to continuously upgrade and change our codes to fortify the entry. The reason the traditional warriors, Nyenplu Taylor and Juezeo Barway, did a lot of killings that the nation could not understand was that all the upgrading and fortifying of our spheres of power required human sacrifices.

I trust by now you understand why I earlier said my priestly role was crucial and critical. The battle kept going against the tribe as old man Swen saw from the realms of the spirit, but we protected the president till his death.

## SPIRITUAL CLUES TO PRESIDENT DOE'S DEATH

The death of the President Doe came about when he desired to satisfy his political contemporaries and the international communities. The president started renewing his relationship with other tribes and made plans to take his birthday celebration to other counties one after the other. He went as far as getting initiated into other cults such as the Poro society, the Masonic craft, and others. Those were the very spiritual powers we had asked him to break with as we entered the power race. I am sure the president's initiation into the Poro societies in 1988 was intended to be a political rite to win the tribes involved with Poro issues. But the Zoes gave him the name Tanue, one of the highest ranks among the Poro ranking, to entrap him. A secret code was assigned to him by the Zoes for easy access. From 1988 until the time of the war, their secret code was of no effect because we were still in charge, and every access to him was closely monitored.

When the war went against us, we were put on the defensive and retreated to the executive mansion and the BTC Barracks in Monrovia. The rest of the country was captured and controlled by Taylor and his forces. The Zoes from the Poro and other crafts had time to fly around the country and reconsolidate themselves against us. Some Zoes and elders from the Poro took this occasion to get back at the president, using General Prince Y. Johnson, the leader of the Independent National Patriotic Front of Liberia (INPFL), the fastest fighting group at the time, as their instrument. The team of Zoes and elders visited General Johnson, based in Coward, a settlement at the outstretch of Monrovia, to disclose to him the secret code and how to use it to capture the president.

It was a shock to us and "breaking news" to the world when General Prince Y. Johnson entered into the BTC Barracks. Talley, one of the traditionalists, tried to have Johnson killed, but the president stopped him, being curious about what prompted the general's audacity. When Johnson reached the president, he gave the normal military salute and the president returned the at-ease. The general then gave a Poro greeting and released the code, making the president open up to the general. He finally hugged the president traditionally. It was then the president promoted him as a general. Before that, "P.Y.J.," as he is widely known in Liberia, was a captain in the armed forces of Liberia.

The purpose of the general's visit was to reactivate the Poro access to the president. After that event, I lost the full spiritual control I previously had over the president. While we were still trying to break off the Poro spiritual control on the president, he woke up one morning and left the executive mansion for Free Port, the peacekeeper's base (ECOMOG—Economic Community of West Africa Monitoring Group), without our advice or knowledge. After General Johnson's encounter with President Doe, he kept monitoring the president both physically and spiritually.

The ECOMOG peacekeepers asked the president, his few bodyguards, and other officials with him to disarm before entering the base in Free Port on September 9, 1990. General Johnson seized this moment of vulnerability to arrest and kill President Doe.

The general repeatedly asked the president for the meaning of his middle initial, K. On several occasions, the president whispered "Kanyon" in response, and that was what everybody in the nation believed the K meant. The general refused to believe it and insisted on the meaning of the name. Finally the president said, "Kwetii," which traditionally means, "the interest of the gods." This secret had been revealed by the Poro elders to the general, because they hated the president for the way he had allowed the traditional leaders and the spirits from the southeast to overshadow and control the political and spiritual atmosphere of the nation.

I do not know fully what these explanations mean, but I want you to understand that spirits are a fighting legacy in, especially African, government, companies, and many other organizations, including families.

## EXILED AND RETURNED

After President Doe was killed, the Krahn tribe retaliated and burned down many houses in the nation. Most members of the tribe fled the country into self-imposed exile. The national influence of our priesthood was threatened. The Interim Government of National Unity (IGNU) was established, and representatives of various factions were placed in government positions. Despite all this, we still held on our tribal influence and spiritual establishment in and outside the country.

The president's death initially threatened my international (West African) priestly post, because my national spiritual influence was the major factor in me gaining that post. However, no other priests had reached up to half of my achievements; and based on that, I retained my post.

After some time, the tribe's members, who were languishing economically in exile, agreed to take their revenge. In 1991, we joined with the Mandingo tribe to form ULIMO (United Liberian Movement for Democracy). The Mandingos were also hunted by Charles Taylor's NPFL men because they supported the Doe regime, which made them Liberian citizens. I did not wholeheartedly give my support to ULIMO, because it was dominated by the Mandingos, who were Muslims. I knew their Islamic religion to be a cult, because each time I made an attempt on them, I met with an impediment that could only be negotiated with their priest. This meant the god they worshiped would ask me to pay a special homage to spiritually exploit them.

As for the people I now know as Christians, I could not negotiate with anybody to exploit them. The marks they carry have no earthly trace, and as a result, no negotiation could be made with any human to exploit them spiritually. The only way I ever succeeded in harming them was if they displayed carelessness in their Christian walk.

By this time, I was only giving protection to individual members of ULIMO, especially members of my tribe. In 1993, there was a split in the group and many Krahn members were brutally murdered. They sought their tribal arm of support, but many did not know how to contact me because most of them had lost their interest in tribal traditions when President Doe was killed. They were finally able to trace and locate me through the help of General J. Apollo Swen Jr., because they knew that his father was also a priest. They came to me for general tribal protection, but I could not give it to them because it was not the season. Instead, I had to take off my priestly garment and reduce my status by putting on a warrior's garment.

As a priest who was consenting to reduce my status, I requested that I should be given the freedom to make as many sacrifices as I deemed necessary. This decision was pleasing to the military leaders, but not to the political leaders because my numerous killings would hinder their political ambitions. It was then decided that I come to the battlefront only when necessary. I came on specific missions, such as the rescue mission for certain tribal members who were held captive by ULIMO-K (the faction of ULIMO led by the Mandingos after the faction split up; ULIMO-J was the faction of the Krahns).

The fracas between ULIMO-J and the ECOMOG began after a faction of the ECOMOG soldiers connived with Mr. Taylor to illegally disarm our boys. They offered our soldiers two bags of rice and two hundred US dollars for each weapon. When the frontline generals became aware of the ECOMOG ulterior motive, they barred ECOMOG from entering their control area. But ECOMOG harnessed their free access to our part of the regiment to spark off an illegal battle. I threw my spiritual weight behind my tribe to enable it to challenge the sophisticated armored tanks of ECOMOG.

## GENERAL BUTT NAKED IN ACTION

My last and greatest challenge as a war general was the conflict termed the "April 6 Fracas." Trouble broke out when Mr. Taylor made efforts to forcefully arrest the leader of the ULIMO-J faction, Major General D. Roosevelt Johnson, on the two-count false charge of illegal storage of arms and murder. General Dugbah,

ULIMO-J's Chief of Staff, and I stood in resistance to the arrest, as did ECOMOG. When Mr. Taylor could not contend with us, he engineered another influential leader of our tribe, General Armah Youlo, to refute the headship of Major General Roosevelt Johnson. General Youlo had just been released from jail in Sierra Leone. He had been jailed for killing General Karpeh, the would-be leader of the entire ULIMO movement, which began in Sierra Leone. General Youlo got all the support needed from Mr. Taylor, drawing virtually all the fighters from his quarters to his side.

The April 6 Fracas began when a man named Dweh Barwu was killed by his own (NFPL) men near Roosevelt Johnson's ULIMO-J headquarters. Dweh was a member of a squad that came down to 19th Street to provoke our soldiers by throwing stones at us, while another squad on the beachway laid ambush for us between 16th and 15th Streets. They knew ECOMOG was not at the beachway. We followed the stone-throwers. Dweh was very brave and stayed behind his men, with our boys right on his heels. His men crossed their firing line and began shooting. Taking Dweh to be one of us, they killed him. After this, all hell broke loose as NPFL and ULIMO-K forces attacked Roosevelt Johnson's house and our men. From there, the war spread throughout the city.

Mr. Taylor blamed General Johnson for the conflict, and held that as grounds to apprehend him. He was supported by a group of women fanatics who had accused us of being the aggressors and gave Mr. Taylor an ultimatum to either remove the "Naked People" from the street or they would remove them, even if it cost them their lives. Seeing that the people did not recognize the true cause of the conflict, we decided it was better to get General Johnson out of the city and fight our way to meet him in the Bomi Hills. Our slogan was "Better dead than blind."

It was at this point that I was set loose from the cage. Even some of the political leaders who had previously opposed me saw they were susceptible to death and that I was the only way out of danger. My first task was to gather weapons. I went to one of our bases in Robertsport for arms, but I was only able to bring five pieces through the sea—one RPG (rocket-propelled grenade), one M-60 machine gun, two G3 machine guns, and one AK-47. My boys and I were about sixty in number and we started the fight with just those five arms—the M-60 and the AK-47 were malfunctioning—while Charles Taylor's fighting men were more than three thousand and fully armed.

We decided to move on some ECOMOG soldiers who were taking care of the John F. Kennedy Hospital, the general government hospital in Liberia. We were able to collect twelve weapons there. From there, we were able to penetrate the group of Charles Taylor's militia from the airport to join forces with our cohorts, the fighting men of the Liberia Peace Council. However, to protect the port and arrange aircraft to carry on our plans, we needed more armament. I decided to disarm the Ghanaian contingent that was guarding the airport.

At first, Roosevelt Johnson offered the commander of the Ghanaian contingent $10,000 US to turn over their arms to us and then report to the authorities that the arms were forcefully taken from them. They turned down the offer. I responded by bringing out a POW we had captured, General Domingo, a Gambian who fought for Mr. Taylor with the agreement that Mr. Taylor would support a rebel movement in Gambia, and ordered my boys to cut him into fifty pieces with an axe in the presence of the Ghana contingent. Immediately, the spirit of fear filled the air and I swiftly capitalized on it, taking seventy-two weapons from the Ghanaians. Disarming them was as easy as drinking water. However, we failed in our attempt to send our leaders to Bomi Hills.

We then decided to retreat to the BTC Barracks, because that was where we had the majority of our tribesmen. Mr. Taylor had plans to massacre our people in the barracks. At this time, I had more than 70,000 people under my priestly protection. I oversaw my people from three different battlefronts, as a mother hen would do for her chicks. My presence at every battlefront was very important, as I was often alerted as to where there was pressure and could run to the rescue.

## THE SPIRIT OF FEAR

Eventually we ran out of the ammunition we had forcefully acquired from the peacekeepers. Bullets from the three fronts were falling on us like rain and our people were dying. The spirit of fear was my last resort, and I did not hesitate to fire it into the air. First, I prepared myself by performing human sacrifices. Then, to garner courage, I told everyone in the barracks to shout and sing praises to my name. Then I went in the midst of the opposite forces with my traditional warring knife. I used the spirit of fear to make the opposite side confused, undecided, and jittery.

One day, a Nigerian colonel marched into our barracks with a contingent of five hundred troops, demanding the release of all international hostages we had been using as human shields. The hostages were the only avenue by which the international community was stopping Charles Taylor from raining his bombshells on our innocent populace. Their mission was to free the hostages and kill our men. Some of the other generals gave up because the troops were many, well-equipped, and tactically positioned.

They commanded all our people in the barracks to lay down in front of the armored tanks that had gained access to us.

Some women ran to my door with their usual cry for help. I asked them to bring me a young baby. They complied by bringing the baby, who was less than a year old. I held the two legs of the baby and burst his head against the wall. The brain and everything in the baby was used to speedily prepare me to cast the spirit of fear upon my enemies.

I walked straight to the Nigerian colonel and, with my finger pointing at his face, demanded the arrest and disarmament of him and his men. Some of the five hundred men were not in my spiritual ring of fear, so a few of them escaped. The rest of them were arrested along with their armored tanks. Swift to action, I commandeered the tank and put it into use against Charles Taylor and his men.

I frequently fought the ECOMOG peacekeeping force whenever I ran out of ammunition, because they would not fight back at any faction unless they had the mandate. But most often I released the spirit of fear into the atmosphere and anyone in range would be subjected to fear and confusion. I thereafter tailored them to my orders.

Though there were many others I disarmed just using the spirit of fear, on two different occasions I met with some resistance I could not withstand. One was a Nigerian ECOMOG captain and his men assigned to inspect the various front lines on which their men were posted. I released my charms of fear and advanced toward the captain. But he rebuffed my threats and told his men not to consent to any act of poaching from my men or myself. The captain also ordered them to fire at us. I was so surprised! To this end, I doubled up the spirit of fear that I had released. I saw these men using their hands and bouncing on their toes; some of them opened and closed their eyes. Then they rounded off in a chorus of, "Amen!" I persisted in marching toward the captain. He even shot several rounds to warn me to steer clear saying, "General, one more step and I will bring you down." I reconsidered and backed off, especially seeing how close his bullets came to me.

The second experience I had was with Major Solomon Okin (now a full colonel) and his men, who also resisted me because they were all strong Christian believers. I finally had to leave the barracks and move to an abandoned building to secure one of the bridges, which was a major access to attack us. The retreat was to create an access point between the factions of Alhaji Kromah and Charles Taylor. I was not comfortable with the crowd at the barracks, as they impeded the flow of my human sacrifices.

# Chapter 5

# TRADING TRIBAL PRIESTHOOD FOR A GOD-HONORING PRIESTHOOD

*But you are a chosen generation, a royal priesthood, a holy nation, His own special people, that you may proclaim the praises of Him who called you out of darkness into His marvelous light* (1 Peter 2:9).

One fateful day, in order to fulfill the customary ritual before battle, I negotiated with the mother of a three-year-old girl to give me her daughter for sacrifice. She accepted my request, and turned the girl over to us. Obviously this is unnatural for a mother who loves her child so dearly to turn her child over for ritual, but that was the effect of the spiritual influence I gained over people. I usually gained it by providing them with food or medications upon which I had cast spells.

My soldiers and I moved to the frontline on the new bridge and started the ritual by opening the little girl's back and plucking out her heart. I shared the little girl's heart with my soldiers. After we ate, I asked my boys to go to the river and bring some water for me to wash my hands.

As I waited for my boys, I heard a voice behind me. "My son, why are you enslaving yourself?" I turned around to see a very bright light, brighter than the sun, and the form of a Man about ten feet tall with a cloud around His feet. I could only look at His feet, because the cloud around His feet reduced the intense brightness of the light. But the rest of His body, which I could not see, was brighter than the sun. One can at least glance at the sun, but I could not behold the brightness of His glorious presence for a moment.

The Man's words made no sense to me. I considered my authority as a general. By then, I had the authority to command anyone to be released, even if his crime deserved death. I could also demand the death of an innocent person in my control area and no one could stop it. So, I responded, "Why are You calling me a slave, when I am supposed to be a king?"

He said, "You rightly said you are supposed to be a king, but you are living like a slave." While I pondered what He meant, He continued. "A king's servant is at his footstool, but your servant is on your shoulder." These words sent a sharp chill through my entire body, such as I had never experienced before.

"What do you mean?" I asked.

He said, "You won't understand anything I am telling you now, but repent and live—or refuse and die." Then He disappeared as my men trooped in with the water.

I stood, mute and dumbfounded, as the raging sound of the battle drew nearer. Very perturbed in my mind, I led my men to the battlefront, the shadow of my real self. I usually shot my pistol as a way to give signals to my men from all corners to approach the battle. On that fateful day, as I shot into the air to draw my men to myself, my pistol exploded. I took my SAG (simple assassin gun) rifle to serve for the signal. It also split open. Finally, I tried my RPG (rocket-propelled grenade), and it exploded. I was demoralized and greatly afraid. I directed my men to retreat and stop the fight. Strangely enough, in the course of leading my troop to the battlefront, a gunshot from an enemy hit me on my tibia (lower leg). The bullet did not penetrate, but my covenant with the Nya-ghe-a-weh as his priest was jeopardized by that singular occurrence. Before that, any bullet shot at me only came within twenty meters of me.

That was the first time I had ever retreated from a battle. Nya-ghe-a-weh was always to the rescue when issues were above my head, making good on his claim to have given me the greatest power. But after my first experience with Christ, followed by the unusual drama with my three different guns, Nya-ghe-a-weh could not show up. I considered the option of laying down arms as well as the battle. I kept away from the frontline. While I was having all of these strange experiences, my men suffered heavy casualties due to my absence. I resolved to do away with anything in relation to the manipulation of Nya-ghe-a-weh, so as to give a second thought to the command I had received to repent.

I cannot explain why I never deemed it fit, nor could summon the courage, to relate my ordeal with the strange voice who called me "son" to Nya-ghe-a-weh when he appeared for his usual visitations and soul trips. I couldn't stop thinking about all the strange things I had experienced on the frontline. It became obvious that my first encounter with Christ had created a spark in the spirit realm. Nya-ghe-a-weh continued to appear for our soul travels every night, but his countenance changed toward me. He appeared very dull, like a man who suspects his wife of having extramarital affairs but has no proof.

# SOUL WINNING

The Soul Winning Evangelical Ministries (SWEM) is a league of inter-denominational ministers and believers who were tired of the brutal consequences of the war and decided to opt for a spiritual warfare campaign against both fighters and warlords through fasting and prayer. The title of their campaign slogan: OPERATION DESTROY EGYPT'S FIRST-BORN. All key players in the war had another rival to reckon with as the Spirit of God took preeminence to destroy anyone who did not abide by the prophetic utterances of the ministers to desist from the war.

In their campaign, SWEM declared Barnesville, a northern suburb of Monrovia, as Goshen, a place of refuge free from arms and mayhem. After Barnesville was spiritually mapped to be a safe haven, two of Charles Taylor's militias entered there on a looting spree. When they were about to snatch a resident's car, somebody ran to the ministers to inform them about the ordeal. "It is not possible," they prophetically declared. After this, weaponless civilians went up to the fighters, disarmed them, and took them to the police station. Chief of Army Staff of the Armed Forces of the Republic of Liberia (AFL) Major General Dumuya intercepted them and had them executed immediately, but by violating the safe haven himself, he became the next person to suffer from ignorance of prophetic declarations. That very day, Dumuya went to the front line leading the Guinea's armored tanks in their attempt to break down the BTC Barracks and capture Roosevelt Johnson at all cost. One of our frontline commanders captured and killed Dumuya.

The Soul Winning ministry also prayed to have me out of the way, and understandably so; I was notorious and acutely dreaded by young and old. Though none of them knew me in person, my war name "General Butt Naked" was more than a household name in Liberia, and among the ECOMOG troops and the international press, with whom I and my troops paraded completely nude on several fronts. My name alone usually sent shocks of terror to other fighters and fronts. My nudity alone painted me not only as mad, but as a sociopath. It was the greatest risk for the outreach ever to think of doing anything to me.

I had no knowledge that a group of Christians were on a vigorous campaign to either destroy me or rescue me from the powers of darkness. These believers were bold to reside in the vicinity of my archenemies, Charles G. Taylor and Alhaji G.V. Kromah while praying for me, a man considered to be a terror to Charles Taylor. Someone found out about this and reported them to the authorities. God miraculously rescued them from the hands of the fighters, and they decided to re-christen me "Joshua" in one of their prayer sessions to hide my identity—the name that stands today as my redemption name. The campaigners conducted fifty-four days of prayer and fasting to win me over to Christ. They were in tune with God and must have heard a sure word from Him, for it is only God who could give them that kind of boldness. That they won me over reveals the power of their sincerity of purpose and spiritual maturity.

My presence in Camp Johnson Road, a street we had commandeered as our base, created great fear in both local residents and infiltrators who sought to use the street as a route to the executive mansion and elsewhere. Fellow fighters who were not assigned to my battalion could not easily play around my vicinity, much less ordinary civilians. Every day my quest for blood rose; but at this point, ECOMOG had declared and was monitoring the cease-fire in Monrovia, so I had no easy access to blood. The sharp fall in my sacrificial lambs made me yearn for blood often. I didn't find it comfortable each time people approached my vicinity, as I was like a hungry lion.

## KNOCK, KNOCK

The Soul Winning Evangelistic Ministries decided to pay me a visit to minister salvation to me. Everyone they told knew they were on a suicide mission. One day, one of their pastors succeeded in reaching my house and knocked at the door. That knock was a knock directly at my heart.

I opened the door to see a casually dressed man, who greeted me, "Jesus loves you, General."

Wondering who he was, I asked him with which language had he greeted me. He responded, "Heavenly language."

I then asked, "And how should I respond?"

"Say 'Amen,'" he replied.

I said, "Amen." I was dumbfounded. I could not grasp why a civilian would ever be brave enough to enter my residence uninvited. I searched for reasons. Perhaps he had come to report my boys for causing some trouble. Maybe he was a journalist, or one of the owners of the house, which I had forcefully taken over. But none of these guesses made sense to me. As I tried to mask my discomfort, he began his conversation by offering me a seat in my own house. I grew increasingly troubled, but I had no desire to do him any harm. He talked about so many things, but I cannot remember any of them because my mind was entirely captivated by his bravery.

At one point, he asked me to close my eyes for him to pray for me. As I did, I remembered a warning from Nya-ghe-a-weh. He had been threatened by Sister Florence, a lady who presently attends the Monrovia Christian Fellowship, when she made it her duty to pray during the riot that sparked up the April 6 Fracas. She cautioned me every day with rhetorical questions, telling me about life and its other sides and meanings. I did not like talking with people once I had prepared for battle, but this unusual woman would always see me and call me by my first name, Milton. Nya-ghe-a-weh, who knew what this woman wanted from me, saw that I was becoming the shadow of what I was as a priest, so he put his deceptive wit to use. He told me that Charles Taylor was going to use "prayer people" to get at me, and warned me against anything about prayer or Christ. However, the flashback on Nya-ghe-a-weh's warning did not convince me to harm the minister before me.

The man brought me back from my memories with a command: "I said, 'Close your eyes and let us pray.'" I spread my fingers over my face in pretense and watched him while he prayed. I had made up my mind to squeeze the life out of him if he tried anything funny. When he finally left, I immediately ran to ask my boys who the guy was.

"Which guy are you talking about, sir?" they asked me.

"Didn't you see the man who just came down these stairs?"

"No sir, we didn't."

"You mean you didn't see the man who just passed here?"

"No sir, we really didn't see anyone."

I became very afraid. My mind went running through the many unusual scenes of the past days. I began to feel miserable and my self-confidence weakened.

The next day, at almost the same time, I heard the same knock at my door and on my heart.

There were two men this time, and their boldness was so much that I could not hide my feelings. But I had no drive to harm them, especially as the second man was smaller than the first in stature. The two of them, Pastor Carr and Pastor Kun Kun, were no threat to me, because just a push could finish them. After that particular visit, I saw them down the stairs to make sure my boys witnessed the presence of the two men. When I asked my boys again, they swore it was the first time they had seen their faces.

In their bid to arrest me spiritually, the Christians began hosting a powerful prayer meeting in a two-story building opposite my house. They intensified their prayers. After these fellowship meetings, they trooped into my house uninvited and declared prophetic words into all nooks and corners of my house, except my bedroom and coven. At the completion of each prophetic utterance, they asked me to say, "Amen." I made my response snappy so they would understand it was time to leave. Another thing I couldn't explain was how the sound of their prayers got into my soundproof coven from across the street. Before that, no volume of sound could affect me while in the coven.

One day they invited me to worship at the fellowship. I unconsciously agreed. Their meeting lasted from 4-6 p.m. A few minutes before the time, they came to remind and invite me. I assured them I would be at the fellowship. I thought I would attend once as a way to get them off my back. As I took my third step down the stairs on my way to the fellowship, Nya-ghe-a-weh appeared and called out to me, "Hero, what are you going to do with those people? Those guys will first make a mockery of you and then destroy you, because they have the power to do so."

I made a fast U-turn and ran back up the stairs to my spiritually fortified home. I got my men ready as if we were going on a mission. I was confused; it was as if I had forgotten that I was within my own territory. I told my men, "If those guys come up here again, do your work" (meaning, kill them immediately).

Strangely, the Soul Winning members who regularly trooped into my house after fellowship without invitation did not surface at my house that day. I concluded that they were really a destructive force. No one knew exactly what I had planned against those prayerful and committed men except the boys in whom I confided.

Three days later, I got a signal from General Roosevelt Johnson that General Victor Malu, a new field commander of ECOMOG, was in town and would be going around for inspection. In compliance with the cease-fire, I issued orders to the boys in my command to disarm and take the ammunition to the armory. That very day, the Soul Winning members trooped into my house for their usual visitation. I confronted them right away. "What have you guys come here to do? You want to destroy me, right? Do you think you will succeed?"

"Oh, General, what are you saying?" one of them asked.

"Do not pretend. You know exactly what I am talking about. You guys have power up there that you want to use and destroy me." With a dominant rhythm of a shrewd general, I further said: "But, maybe you guys have not heard about me, the original Brigadier General Butt Naked, the one who dealt with General Alhaji Kromah in Bomi Hills. Didn't you hear about me in Weasua, and my bravery in German Camp?" I gave a serious laugh. "Charles Taylor is my wife. I'm the only one who subdued ECOMOG. I'm the original General Butt Naked! No other Naked but me."

All my boasting was intended to discourage and frighten them. I felt my words had fallen on fertile ground. But then, the dismissive expression on Pastor John Kun Kun's face, which bloomed with smiles, watered down my threats. With a soft Liberian intonation, he said, "My man, we do really have power! But our powers will not destroy you. They will help you, chief."

The words left a hole in my heart. I was broken with shame, and I said, "Whether your powers help or don't help, you shouldn't ask after me."

After the drama subsided, Pastor Kun Kun, again with a soft, respectful tone that betrayed no fear of my fame or authority, said, "General, let's bow our heads for prayer, as we are about to leave."

Never had I seen such a persistent character in a group of people. They were more determined for a single soul than the group of desperate warriors I led. The most unbearable experience I had with the Soul Winners Evangelistic Ministry was when I got embarrassed by the prayers of their members, especially the one I described as militant, Pastor Samuel Carr, who came almost twice a day, and later invited me again to attend fellowship. Evangelist Richard Clarke also began to visit me.

## THE FALL OF NYA-GHE-A-WEH

The night before my second invitation to fellowship with the Soul Winning Evangelistic Ministries was when the actual battle was won in the spirit. That night was the first in fourteen years that I didn't receive my usual 12-4 a.m. visitation from Nya-ghe-a-weh. I always went to bed early in order to awake at 10:00 p.m., giving me two hours to prepare my soul for soul travel with Nya-ghe-a-weh at 12:00 a.m. With the cease-fire on, I had nothing to do that leisure day, so I entered my room at about 6:00 p.m. to sleep. As I sat on my bed, I was instantly caught up in a trance. The roof above me opened, and I watched with astonishment as the clouds began to part. I saw floating dew in a thick bank of cloud descending and pouring on my forehead. The pores all over my skin began spilling out black smoke. This continued until the morning, until I was like a heavy log saturated in water lying on my bed.

About 3:00 in the afternoon the next day, Richard Clarke came to inquire about me. "Is he still sleeping?"

"Yes, the chief is still sleeping."

My boys dared not allow anyone to come near my door, nor talk of waking me up. It was customary for me to wake or come out in my own time. I was greatly relieved when I heard my boys tell Richard Clarke that I was still in bed. I had yet to come to terms with the voice that called me "son," the outburst of gunfire on the day of battle, and the outpouring of dew on my forehead. I had thought of relating all the weird mishaps to Nya-ghe-a-weh, but I always forgot. I also thought he should be intervening on my behalf, especially in supernatural situations like the one I had just had, which surpassed human understanding. "Maybe those guys have an answer to it all," I wondered. "But what could be the reason Nya-ghe-a-weh is keeping me at arm's length with those guys?"

Right there and then I made up my mind to attend the fellowship that night. I was taking my bath when Richard knocked at the front door. His voice was audible. "Has he woken up?"

"We don't know."

"Go and wake him up. We have an appointment with him."

In their usual protective way, my boys asked, "What kind of appointment do you have with the chief that will warrant us intruding into his privacy and waking him up from his rest?"

But before they could conclude the questioning, Brother Clarke came to the door of my room and knocked, saying, "General, the meeting has started and I came for you." I told him to wait for me, as I was almost through. But when I realized that I was going against Nya-ghe-a-weh, I decided to wait, and said to Brother Clarke, "Go ahead, I will come for the fellowship." The relentless effort and courage of Brother Clarke struck me. I made up my mind to be part of the service, not because I wanted to be a Christian, but to see what they did at the fellowship and to confirm if they had a hand in my strange experiences.

As I crossed the road to attend the fellowship, Nya-ghe-a-weh appeared again to intercept me. This time he spoke in a weak and powerless tone. He reminded me of my yearnings to be great and whined, "Hero, where are you going?"

I was astonished at the sudden loss of his oratorical skills. Lots of things ran through my mind in quick succession. I was very curious to determine the true identity of these new confidants who Nya-ghe-a-weh gave stern warning about. I remembered all the triumphant battles I had fought, and yet somehow these harmless men could make Nya-ghe-a-weh uncomfortable. As I reflected on Nya-ghe-a-weh's promise to make me the greatest man in my generation, I came between two options—to throw my weight behind Nya-ghe-a-weh and be limited in my greatness, or test the danger of those men and the strength of Nya-ghe-a-weh's protection.

I finally decided, and made myself clear to the ancient deceiver of my tribe: "I am going up there!" I pointed up to the room where Soul Winning was fellowshipping. Nya-ghe-a-weh instantly trembled and fell as I spoke those words. Despite his effort to stand aloof, he fell backward as if something heavy was pushing him down. He cried, "Hero, do you realize what you are turning our bond into? Please change your mind and don't go up there."

This experience opened my eyes to the greatness of the power of human will. After my bold utterance to the ancient god of my forefathers and the humiliation he suffered in my hands, I became afraid, and ran up to the fellowship for protection from any retaliation by Nya-ghe-a-weh.

As I was about to enter the fellowship, I saw an angel standing at the right side of the door. Because I knew the difference between spirit being and human being, I bowed to worship as a sign of my allegiance to the angel, thinking that the angel was their God. But the angel refused my worship, saying he was only there to take record of the people entering the service and to observe their commitment to Christ. He then pointed to Pastor Kun Kun and said he was the man who would lead me to the One I was supposed to worship. He told me to obey him in all that he commanded me to do, and believe him.

I then entered the hall, and contrary to Nya-ghe-a-weh's claims that I would be a laughingstock, ashamed and disgraced by the people, members of the fellowship received me warmly. They made me feel as if my presence in the service meant more to them than the purpose for which they were gathered as Christians or members of the fellowship. It was as if someone had announced that there was no more war in Liberia. Members of the fellowship went on hugging one another after everyone had welcomed me into the assembly of believers with songs and dance.

Pastor John Kun Kun was called on to deliver the message. The message was entitled, "Dangerous Christianity." Its quotations and scripture references are still fresh in my memory, even though I was not familiar with Bible quotations and standard expressions when I heard it. In that historic meeting the pastor stressed:

1. That a Christian should not be a coward.

2. How Christians become victims of others' decisions when they refrain from involvement in the socioeconomic culture of their nation.

3. Christians should be bold, persistent, and courageous.

He held the Church in Liberia responsible for the war because they had everything necessary to stop the war, but resorted to taking sides. By siding with the unforgiving spirit, they were not as powerful as they ought to be. Then he described how he had experienced Christ's power firsthand—how he had disappeared and walked through dangerous paths, and how he had made dangerous utterances to witches that they couldn't oppose. He recited the prophetic utterance and decree pronounced on their base, Barnesville. Pastor Kun Kun concluded by saying that those powers were paid for by their Lord Jesus but Christians do not put the powers in use.

By that point, I was willing to do everything to be part of them. At the end of the message, he made an altar call, which I examined and retained with my spiritual insight. He said, "If there is anyone here who wants to give his or her life to Jesus, please come up." Though the word sounded sweet and familiar to members of the fellowship, I saw it as harmful, because my mind was reflecting on my past activities. I had given lives for powers I needed, so I dare not give my life to anyone. Then the Holy Spirit admonished the pastor to paraphrase his altar call in a simple form. He said, "If anyone in this meeting wants to join us, please come forward."

I got up, marched to the pulpit with a submissive heart, and declared my intention of changing hands from my old master. I was told to repeat words after the pastor, words I later came to know as the "sinner's prayer," declaring my confession, willingness, and readiness to serve Jesus Christ. Though I said the prayer with excitement and a firm desire to serve a new master, I really had no idea *who* I was making a covenant with or becoming part of.

As I recited the last words of the sinner's prayer, I instantly fell prostrate in the Spirit. As I fell, I was caught up into another world, which I later learned to be the Spirit realm. I saw an angelic Person, but He was far superior to men and angels. He appeared bold and full of authority. I remembered my first encounter with the Man who appeared to me on the battlefront at New Bridge. As I was still slain in the Spirit, with the influence of the fellowship members binding and raining prayers of all kinds on me, I tried to recall that first encounter. He softly interrupted my reflection, and said, "Exactly, You have seen me before." He was dressed in a linen robe with a key flying in His hand. He said, "I was the One who told you, 'You are a king, but you are living like a slave.'"

I wanted to explain the covenant I had made with Nya-ghe-a-weh. I began to stutter, but He stopped me, as if to say my past was of no relevance to Him. The key in His palm was now between His index finger and thumb as He said, "This is the key of life. I am the Owner of this key and am in full control of it. Nya-ghe-a-weh told you never to cease making human sacrifices to him for the powers given you, and never to tell anyone things that transpired between you and him. He also said you would die if you eat or touch kola nuts. But I am now saying you will not die, but live and expose him, because I want you to. If anyone joins My company, I take full control of them. Therefore, go into the world and expose Nya-ghe-a-weh as I will inspire and lead you." He continued, "You don't need the life of another man to live. I'm the Provider of life and its totality. Go and tell the world about his deception."

I carefully listened to all He said, still slain in the Spirit, with the members of Soul Winners circling me. He continued His speech with authority. "You were told by Nya-ghe-a-weh, the god, not to eat or touch kola nuts or you would die. I say, since it is the most common of your taboos, you can eat kola nuts to tell who is lying between Me and him."

In the spirit, I could see my body lying lifeless beside the group of the fellowship members. Then the Lord commanded me: "Do it as you return. He has only succeeded in deceiving you because his picture is greatly carved in your mind. My followers are not so effective today, because My picture is not carved in their minds like the picture of Nya-ghe-a-weh's was carved in yours." Finally, he said, "Go and tell the world about the vision you have seen of Me, and tell them I truly exist."

After this, I saw myself entering my body in a slow pace. With exceeding great joy and excitement, I woke up and exclaimed, "Leave me! Nya-ghe-a-weh can do nothing to me!" The fellowship members were attempting to deliver me from the dark world through prayers and tightly held me as I fought to rise up. Then Pastor John Kun Kun sharply interrupted, "Leave him."

When they released me, I jumped up and ran downstairs to authenticate His revelation.

Everyone, including the Soul Winners, upon seeing one of the most famous, brave, and crafty generals running quickly down the street waving my arms thought I was going mad. Eyewitnesses looked with mouths agape. The deliverance team began running behind me as I went from corner to corner and table to table searching for kola nuts to eat, so I could nullify the covenant I made with Nya-ghe-a-weh and establish the truth that my new Master was superior.

I saw a mini market near a female peddler's house and grabbed some kola nuts. Members of the Soul Winners observed me curiously. For a moment, as my hand held the kola nuts close to my mouth, I contemplated whom to obey. Suddenly, with total relief, I vividly remembered His words during my encounter with Him, "Do it as you return." I started eating the kola nuts one after the other like a hungry man, as if my life depended on it. I finished the whole pan of 70 Liberian dollar's worth. The lady left all her goods and ran like the Samaritan woman at the well to inform the residents that I, General Butt Naked, was going mad.

News about my madness spread like wildfire. Carried away with excitement, I started singing, "If you think I'm crazy, then I'm crazy for Jesus!" In the face of the drama, my bodyguards ran to our leader, General Roosevelt Johnson, to inform him that I had gone berserk, and asked him to come to my rescue. Nobody likes their priest or oracle going mad. It ignited a deep worry in the minds and actions of the residents, my men, our leader, and other political top brass of the tribe. They thought I should pick a scapegoat to calm myself down, as was my usual practice. Given the cease-fire, General Roosevelt Johnson thought that my sudden disorderliness was the result of the fact that I did not offer my usual sacrifice to the god. He advised that I be taken to Bomi Hills to perform my usual sacrifice and appease the god.

Rather, I returned to the fellowship in high spirits. "I can now eat kola nuts and will not die," I said with a loud voice. (Some people thought I was going insane from killing so many people during the war.) I then appealed to the Soul Winners to guide me in continuing to fight Nya-ghe-a-weh, should he put up a fight because I denounced his covenant. I knew how to invoke Nya-ghe-a-weh's presence and action, but I didn't yet know how to invoke the power of Jesus to impede the oracle from harming me. "Just say 'the Blood of Jesus' or the 'Holy Ghost fire,'" they exclaimed. Without delay, I began to recite: "The Blood of Jesus! The Blood! Holy Ghost fire!"

When the meeting ended, my excitement continued, but the activities of my past also grievously haunted me like a shadow. My old instincts were still there. "Can't you see Charles Taylor's men coming to attack us?" I'd suddenly say, jerking anyone near me in an attempt to either save him or give him a military treat for his carelessness. When I became troubled by my dreadful past, I took to reciting, "The Blood of Jesus! The Blood! Holy Ghost fire!"

After the first day of my conversion in the fellowship, I received regular teaching from Pastor Samuel Carr and others to strengthen me, as I was like a newborn baby in my new faith. A week from my conversion, Monday, happened to be my birthday. The Soul Winners, who met every Monday, decided to celebrate my birthday during the service in honor of my new birth. The message preached at the meeting emphasized salvation. I recited the sinner's prayer again before them all and denounced Nya-ghe-a-weh with great boldness.

Then the leader called me out for a special prayer, similar to an initiation rite. As I bowed for prayer, they stretched forth their hands at me to pray and rebuke all satanic influences over me. When they started to pray, I felt a strange power upon me, and they had to hold me to keep me calm. I began to speak in tongues as the pastors held my hands in prayer and deliverance. That night, I received six different gifts. I spoke in tongues, interpreted tongues, prophesied, ministered healing, and received words of knowledge and words of wisdom. All these gifts were manifested during my first service.

None of the Soul Winning team had ever called me Joshua, the name they gave me while interceding for my conversion. I received a revelation from the Spirit of God and said, "I am hearing someone calling me 'Joshua.'" Immediately, members of the fellowship started rejoicing, jumping, and giving God the glory. This was a revelation in Barnesville. I continued to manifest strange revelations and powers. When I laid my hands on my sick aunt's head, she was healed immediately. One of the pastor's wives started speaking in tongues, and I began to interpret as she spoke: "The battle had just started. The ministry should focus effort and more time in nurturing Joshua. Remember, I told you he is My sign to nations."

I then said to Brother Richard Clarke, "The Lord wants you to know that He only used you to be a guide unto me. Do not take pride in it or try to take the glory. He is God; He has given you the boldness and enablement." Brother Clarke then broke down and gave God the glory. In that meeting so many people were delivered. Many who were not faithful became faithful, and many who were not saved got saved. The presence of God was strong in that service for deliverance, healing, and to strengthen the believers.

## I SURRENDERED MY WEAPONS

While the birthday celebration was going on, I went into my coven and brought out all my equipment, including my guns. I also brought out the traditional throne which I sat on to perform my ritual—it was round and shaped like an Ashanti stool. Strangely, the priestly knives that some members of the PRC used to kill the late President William R. Tolbert Jr. disappeared. The cow tail I used during the war to disperse bullets and rockets also disappeared. The believers refused the weapons and suggested that I should take them to my field commander, the one who gave them to me, since they were pastors and not military personnel.

In a very vocal mood, I marched to the home of the field commander and saluted him to make my presentation. "Sir! I have found a new and better Commander. I'm enlisted in a new army." As I boldly said these words, Johnson wore a sudden frown, suspicious that I was defecting to another faction, precisely, the NPFL of Charles Taylor, as had J. Apollo Swen and others. I then said, "My new Commander is Jesus Christ. These are your arms and ammunition."

He replied with a shrewd smile. I believe his smile was to corroborate what he had heard about my sudden insanity. As I turned over the arms and ammunition, I signaled goodbye and marched out.

"Come, General!" he called after me. "Come, General! Come! I have a small thing here for you!"

"Keep your small thing, sir! Man shall not live by bread alone," I shouted back in response, holding my hands up.

Immediately, I took to my heels. After I left the general's house, I ran to one of the major streets in Monrovia called Broad

Street to purchase a microphone and begin solo evangelism. Strangely, my first experience in the healing ministry was with a mad woman who was completely nude. After I prayed for her, as the spirit led me, my words to her were, "Go home and put on your clothes." She began to weep and opened up to me that she came from a far place. Thereafter, I appealed to sympathizers to give her a cloth to cover her nakedness. She was eventually led to my house where she bathed and was clothed.

## Chapter 6

# RESTORATION BEGINS

My desire to tell the world about Christ and my experiences with the dark world grew in me passionately. I went to one of the biggest markets in a community called Red Light. The community is situated in the eastern suburb of Monrovia in the territory of Charles Taylor. I told those in Red Light about the marvelous thing Christ did for me. I started by telling them of the people I killed during my priesthood and the civil war. I spoke in utter sobriety and appealed to my audience to please forgive me. I also declared that it was time for the other soldiers to join me in the heavenly train to glory, because I was now a new man.

Groups of Charles Taylor's former fighters came to me and threatened to avenge the death of their colleagues. Since I knew the power of the God who had forgiven me, I laughed at them and said, "When I had only eighteen men as personal body guards you were unable to capture me. Now that I have more than 2,000 men with me, what can you do?" (I was referring to the uncountable angels that would usually come around me whenever Nya-ghe-a-weh tried to hurt me.)

Tempers rose and the men quickly ran to the market and began pulling off the table legs to hit me. I stood undaunted, and I pointed my hand toward the fierce mob. I shouted, "Arrest them in Jesus' name!" The market women ran toward the direction of the protesting men like honeybees. They challenged them with these words, "This man killed as you all did, but decided to change and ask for forgiveness. Why can't you reason with him and do the same?" The women stressed that if all the major players of the war could emulate me, the fight would be over. But the men persisted in their action and kept destroying the tables with the intent to attack me. They were so confused that they fought over one another's table legs.

The market women got annoyed and turned against the protesters. When I saw how the market women attacked Taylor's former fighters, I said, "Now you see, my angels have not yet shown up and yet this place is in disarray." The women guarded me through the jam-packed crowd, flagged down a taxi and issued a serious warning to the driver to take me straight to my house. They warned him that he would be responsible, should anything happen to me. I sat at the owners' corner like the king that I am and went to my house.

## CHALLENGES

My first challenge was to leave the territory of my people for Barnesville, which was then in Charles Taylor's control and policed by one of his strong commandos, General Montgomery. I managed to move to Barnesville and lived in Pastor Kun Kun's house without any money. Pastor Kun Kun and the rest of the brethren took care of my daily needs, because everything

I looted I had returned to its legitimate owners, including cars, money, and houses, for which the owners brought legitimate documents to prove ownership.

Another notable challenge was reconciling with members of my family, especially my mother and brothers, who did not know anything about my priestly role and unusual powers. They just found out one day that the dreaded General Butt Naked everyone was talking about happened to be their son and brother.

## TO NIGERIA

Colonel Solomon Okin, a major in the ECOMOG peacekeeping mission from Nigeria, arranged a Nigerian military jet to convey us (Pastor John Kun Kun, Pastor Julius Dennis, gospel artist Brother Kpan, and me) to Nigeria through Colonel Ben Obasa, the chief military intelligence officer under the General Victor Malu administration.

While we were on our way to Nigeria in the aircraft, an ECOMOG captain was used by the devil to tempt me. The captain, who had collected our passports, revealed that if I got to Nigeria, he would report to the authorities that I was a terrorist on a mission in Nigeria. Nya-ghe-a-weh offered me ways to escape if I wished to. I could either jump out of the plane through a window, or threaten the pilot to turn the aircraft back. I was so confused. I went into the bathroom to ponder the option of jumping through a window. Thankfully, the Holy Spirit ministered to Pastor Kun Kun to come after me in the bathroom and counsel me. He came in and prayed with me, and I chose neither plan of escape, though the pressure on me only subsided when we landed in Lagos on December 23, 1996. Pastor Kun Kun went to meet the captain, thanked him for keeping our passports, and asked him to tell us how to find Winners Chapel. We were taken to Winners Chapel with a letter of introduction that Colonel Okin gave us to give the bishop, who was expecting us.

We arrived at Winners Chapel at noon. Just then, daredevil robbers attacked the street, and Nya-ghe-a-weh appeared and challenged me to prove my new shield. I rejected him by going to stop the armed robbers, naïvely trying to jump over the fence to face them. Pastor Kun Kun and Pastor Julius held me down and prayed for me.

The next day, I briefly gave my testimony in the service and necessary arrangements were made for me to be under the auspices of the bishop. However, the Lord directed us to Pastor Salas, who God later used to conduct my physical deliverance. Through that deliverance I vomited out the cowry shells planted in me as remote controls to my eleven different powers.

## MY RETURN TO LIBERIA

My challenges continued when I returned to Liberia. One day, I preached on the roadside. Everyone listening was near tears after hearing my story. But a young man, who was selling petrol by the roadside, walked out of his selling spot and said, "You expect me to listen or believe you after you killed my entire family and even tried to kill me? The very God you are blaspheming saved me, and now you are hiding under Him." I begged him to hear me, but he threatened me more and warned me not to touch him. He said my touching him might lead to me killing him the way I killed his other family members.

Another challenge came from a woman who called me on a radio program and condemned T-Max, the journalist who had invited me on his talk show. The woman said I had raped her and her sisters. The woman later met me in Brewerville when she heard that I was to go there. Her bitter remarks and expression can never leave my memory.

Another brother, whose father I killed by burning him in their house, nearly split my head open with an axe. He noticed me passing in front of the same house where I burned his father. He ran to a corner, waited for me to pass, and lifted the axe. His shadow with the raised axe in his hand rose up before me, so I leapt forward quickly and turned to look at him. He appeared to be frozen. When I gazed to observe him closely, his eyes revealed anger and hatred. I was speechless and spread my two hands before him. "Brother, whatever I have done to you, I am sorry," I said in tears. He also started weeping. Through his tears he said, "How could you pass in front of this house in which you burned the owner, who was my father?" He dropped the axe and kept crying. He told me not to come closer when I tried to console him.

Also at ELWA Junction, I came across Mammy's mother (the little girl whose bride price I paid to legally gain access to her spirit and kill her). Her mother happened to be one of the people in my audience during one of my public confession meetings. In that meeting, I explained how I had used the little girl for the sacrifice. After that, whenever Mammy's mother saw me, she would always break down crying. Mammy was her only daughter, and her death was always fresh in her mother's memory. After the meeting, I tried to explain the circumstances surrounding Mammy's death, but it only awakened her pain and she became very violent. The crowd had to hold her back so as to shield me from the outcome of her wrath.

After that incident, several people advised me to watch my words while giving my testimonies, as the wounds I had inflicted on people were still very fresh in my victims' and their loved ones' memories. As wise as these concerned people's advice may have seemed, I just could not hold back myself. The zeal to narrate and win souls for God overshadowed me.

After some time, I went to Akwa Ibom State in Nigeria to acquire some education at the Church of God Theological Institute, but I could not cope because it was based solely on academic exercises. However, the bishop in charge decided to have me train with other pastors in their churches; as my letter of introduction had informed him that it was not safe for me to return to Liberia. But the Lord appeared to me later and gave me a word for my nation. He asked me to go back to Liberia and tell the nation not to vote for any of the warlords. The Lord also showed me the consequences that would occur if they repudiated this wise counsel.

I returned to Liberia and delivered the message three days before the elections that led Charles Taylor to the presidency.

## CHALLENGES IN EXILE

When I first went to the Budumburam Refugee Camp in Ghana in 1997 to give my testimony, the church in Budumburam had to solicit the help of the police to save my life. It happened that some of the people who escaped from Liberia because of my nefarious activities came to listen to my testimony. In revenge, they mobbed me, hoping to execute jungle justice against me. People from my tribe were also in the crowd and decided to kill me in order to stop me from revealing their culture any further.

No man can run away from his past. He must face it and deal with it. I finally escaped and later returned to the camp in 1998. The same people who shouted "Crucify him!" were now singing "Hosanna." There were still a few detractors—one particular young man said he would never listen to me, though I was invited to the church where he worshiped. I did not do anything to him directly, but he had seen me when I killed a whole family. He walked out of the service as I spoke.

One day, a brother and a friend introduced me to Reverend Harry Truth Warner II, who later assisted me in the cause of publishing this book in Liberia. He said, "There is a girl you have to meet. She has vowed with the last drop of blood in her veins never to forgive you. She showed me the mark of a knife on her thigh. She says that you stopped her trading and stabbed her with a knife." He brought me to meet her, and I could sense the bitterness in her by the way she spoke.

A friend and I went to Nigeria to see General Victor Malu, the Nigerian Army Chief of Staff and former ECOMOG Field Commander. We were kidnapped by a Nigerian soldier who was an ex-ECOMOG personnel in the peace mission in Liberia, and taken to NAFIC, a military barracks in Oshodi. There I was accused of killing the solder's brother and being responsible for his friend's leg being amputated in the incident where the five hundred ECOMOG troops were arrested.

I once was on my way to Ivory Coast for a crusade in Guiglo. Our bus broke down in a town called Dailowa, so we had to spend a night there. There was a woman in the bus who suggested that we lodge in a mini hotel in the community, but since she was a woman, I refused. A little girl heard us talking, and excitedly asked us if we were Liberians. She lived in the town with her mother, who was married to a jardaime marine (police officer). She was very excited to know that we were Liberians, and she took us to her mother. The lady received us and even joyfully cooked for us. Since I was introduced as a pastor, she ushered me into her room while they slept in the little girl's bedroom.

The next morning, this happy woman began to cry. I tried to calm her down, but failed. She prepared our food and asked me to eat, but as I looked at the face of the girl I came with, she looked guilt-stricken. I did not have the slightest idea as to what the problem was. I also refused to take the breakfast she had prepared, but she insisted that I should eat. Not wanting to add salt to her injury, I ate the breakfast. After the breakfast, we started off to continue our journey. The little girl saw us off. I inquired from the sister with us, and she said the woman cried throughout the night after she told her that I was the former General Butt Naked. So I went back to the lady and persuaded her to talk to me. She then related an incidence that occurred in a place called MKK Yard. Immediately, I recollected the incident and scenes of the blood I wasted there. I became lifeless with remorse.

Another incident occurred when I was in Life Tabernacle Church, led by Pastor Oliver Kpan. I was asked to greet the church for a few minutes. When I introduced myself, I saw a lady get up and walk out through the door. After the service, a girl about eighteen years old walked up to me and asked, "Are you really who you said you are? Are you really General Butt Naked?" I said yes, and she said, "When you introduced yourself, my mother who was sitting by me walked out. She asked me to follow her, but I refused and said I wanted to have a talk with you. I was a child when you killed my father." She then described the incident.

Alongside these difficult exchanges, there have been many of my victims who have forgiven me. I tell you, beloved, I cannot explain what has transformed my former victims and touched their hearts to make me the love of their lives today. Most of the time I would only kneel down, surrender myself, and appeal to them in the spirit of genuine repentance and in tears. A few moments later, what takes over them I cannot explain.

Another event that caused the whole nation to accept me was my presence there during the September 18, 1998 Fracas. When people saw me giving my testimony, many saw it as another deception. Some of them compared me to General Prince Y. Johnson, who used to dance to his guitar while singing "Oh, How I love Jesus" and "Because He First Loved Me," after which he would shoot someone in the head. Many expected me to behave in the same way. But eventually they believed me more, especially after the September 18 war came and I did not take part in it.

The war caught up with me at a crusade that very September 18, which was a Friday. I had a preaching engagement in the Ark of Jesus Christ, led by Pastor Chris Crayton. I was also committed to preaching every day at different locations in minicrusades. During my preaching in Red Light Market, the same place where the angels had fought for me, we heard shooting coming from an area close by and saw people running in disarray. Pastor Chris's church was not far from that area of the town, and there was traffic congestion at the double breach, Steven Tolbert Estate, because security men were checking every car. I decided to wait for the meeting at Chris's church instead of trying to go home.

The battle continued that whole night. General Roosevelt Johnson had to escape through the American Embassy, and Charles Taylor captured many great generals. After my message, we used that day in the church to pray for many things in the nation. We did not really know what exactly was going on, but one of the members of the church who was working at the executive mansion told Pastor Chris not to allow me go home on Saturday morning, because Charles Taylor had arrested and killed everybody he saw as threat to him. Pastor Chris then took me to his house along with some other pastors and made arrangements for me to leave the country.

A journalist from Kiss FM (Charles Taylor's station) reported that I was seen fighting. He manipulated the audience to testify that they saw me naked and was fighting again. This was a mockery to my two years of ministry preaching in the name of the Lord Jesus Christ. As I was praying, the Lord showed me that the arrangement the pastors were making to help me escape would damage my testimony. So I told them the best thing for me to do was to go home, which was the craziest suggestion because the entire road was blocked. Charles Taylor's men had mounted checkpoints. There were three different checkpoints on the road to my house.

While discussing this plan, a friend of the pastor drove in with an NGO (non-governmental organization) car, so the pastor asked his friend to drop me off since he was going only a few meters away from my house. I spent the day in the company of the pastors and then we traveled that night, but they were still afraid because of the news from the media. Although I told them where I was, the media propaganda against me was too strong. That night, I remembered the message Pastor Kun Kun preached on the night I received Christ. I declared myself invisible and committed myself to God, because I was about 2,000 meters from my house at the point where the man dropped me off. The pastor never told him who I was.

While I was walking the rest of the way home, many patrol cars of Charles Taylor's men passed by me. Then one of their green jeeps passed by me and then stopped about 200 meters away from me. They reversed and stopped again to look at me through the car's window. The only thing I heard from the car was, "I know the man well, I told you it was not him." They drove off. I got to the house and met Josie (who later became my wife), my mother, other relatives and friends who were all confused and almost mourning for me. They all became excited once they realized it was me and started praising God. I told them my God was in control, and I narrated the rest of the story of how He saved me. We all slept in the house.

The next morning was Sunday, and I had another preaching engagement in Brewerville. To get there, I had to pass through about ten check points. Everyone tried to discourage me from going, but I went. My mind was made up. When I got to the church, the rumor that I had gone back to fight had already been spreading in the church. When I met the pastor who invited me, Henry Moore, at the junction, he told me the church was so discouraged when they heard about my going back, though he himself did not believe it.

That Sunday I preached on "Effective Generational Transfer," after which I returned to the Don Steward Pentecostal Church at Point Four Junction, Bushrod Island, so I could arrange with Pastor Torbor Dixon to borrow their instruments for the next day. He was not comfortable with me carrying the instruments amid all the disorder, but Pastor Moore was one of his pastors who guaranteed use of them. By nine o'clock, Pastor Moore had already set the instruments on Broad Street. I got there and started preaching after about ten minutes. Journalists from various radio stations came to air me live. I announced to the nation that I could not "return to my vomit." If anyone said they saw me fighting, they were right, but they saw me fighting not for Johnson, but for Jesus.

Then I said, "Really, they looked into the spirit realm and saw me fighting that very Friday night. They wanted to know who I was fighting for. They concluded for Johnson because they saw the first letter 'J,' but the 'J' they saw was followed by 'ESUS' and not 'OHNSON.'"

After that the Spirit of God led me to Congo Town, where the radio station that had lied about me was located. The station was about 150 meters from the residence of Charles Taylor, which was crowded with many ATU security men. I marched through them, walked into the radio station, and demanded a rebuttal, which was granted.

Twelve days after the September 18 Fracas was September 30, my birthday. On that day I took my wife out to dinner as a birthday gift. After that, I finally left the country with the assistance of a friend, Pastor David N. Greene, who planned crusades all along the road from Monrovia to Ivory Coast in some major towns along the way. That was the channel by which I left the country of Liberia during the Second Civil War.

## CONFRONTING THE TRIBAL MEN

After the tribe did their utmost to get through to Nya-ghe-a-weh without me but failed, people started dying in the process. So they decided getting to me at all cost. When their repeated messages for me to turn over their priesthood, which would mean my death, went unanswered, they sent a team of elders and traditional warriors to the late General Teh Quiah, my uncle. He sent for me because we were close.

The warriors waited in one room while Chief Kieh Fallay, the head of the council of chiefs and elders, waited for me in the sitting room. I saw my uncle's car and his bodyguards, so I assumed he was in, climbed the stairs and entered his apartment. The chief tried to prostrate and greet me as usual, but I told him that greeting was not meant for me anymore. With the zeal of my new birth in Christ Jesus, I said to him, "If you had not heard about my conversion, please know it now. I am no longer a priest to Nya-ghe-a-weh. I am now a priest of Jesus Christ."

The old man laughed and agreed with me, but he said, "Why don't you first come with us and turn over our priesthood formally. Remember, the war has not ended. We are still being hunted and killed. We cannot get to our forefathers because the god is angry with the tribe for your sake. He is killing those trying to get to him by themselves. Please come with us and the ones the forefathers had kept through times." His pathetic face brought sorrow to my heart as I remembered the tribe and how they were being rejected by every other tribe in the nation.

I tried to reason with them on the need for a priest, saying, "I really don't have anything to turn over, but you would not believe me."

He spread his hands before me and said, "What about the priestly stool, the knife and other symbols of authority?"

I said, "When Jesus arrested me, He confiscated everything I had. The truth is, after my conversion, I went to check for those items, and I could not find them. If you people really need them back, you should get to Nya-ghe-a-weh and he could get them from Jesus, because they are all in the same world."

To him it sounded like I was mocking him, but it was not so. I was being very sincere. But the group of young traditional warriors and other elders listening to us from the other room came to us in the parlor with grim faces and sticks in their hands. They planned to beat me until I became helpless, so they could carry me off to do what they wanted. I could do nothing to that group of strong and gigantic young men because they were in all readiness to appease their forefathers and save the tribe.

It was the grace of God that saved me. Through the wisdom God gave me, I always went about with kola nuts in my bag. Knowing that they were not to touch kola nuts as warriors, I brought out a bunch of kola nuts and threatened to throw them at them if they insisted on attacking me. The whole of them stepped back. "What is Blahyi doing?" they asked. "He has actually planned to destroy our entire heritage."

I walked out of the room, went downstairs, and I started preaching on the main street, while the men watched me from the porch upstairs. I looked up at them and said, "Look how foolish you are. You know me as your priest, and if any one mustn't touch kola nuts, I should be the first. You see me holding kola nuts and yet you are afraid to touch them. While it is true that this very kola has killed a lot of priests and it was used to weaken and destroy a lot of warriors, the One who created it, created you and me. He has given me the right; and I can not only touch it, but watch me as I eat it." Immediately I put the kola nuts in my mouth and started eating them.

I continued, "I know you all trust Nya-ghe-a-weh so much, and he has never failed you from the days of your fathers till now. But let me tell you, he is a deceiver and a wicked man."

They started looking at one another, and some of them even closed their ears to what they considered an abomination. I screamed Nya-ghe-a-weh's name as a weapon against them. "You yourselves have given Nya-ghe-a-weh a lot of blessing. You gave him your cows, your goats, and the harvest of your labor as homage, but your sons or any other person will die if they just touch any of those things you gave to him as gifts. For example, when the people were leaving the city to seek refuge in the town, innocent children who did not hold the tradition in high esteem because they did not understand it were killed for a little goat they ate in hunger. But the same goats, cows, pots of rice, and chickens were eaten by Charles Taylor's men when they captured your area. If your so-called Nya-ghe-a-weh was powerful, why didn't he kill them?"

Many of them saw reason, not only by those statements I made and the kola nuts I ate, but by the Spirit of God who filled that place when I started praying. Sadly, the few who gave their lives to Christ that day went back to the interior because we could not maintain them financially. They were "tried traditionally and killed" by their traditional tribunal.

## RETRIEVING THE FLAG AND SEAL OF LIBERIA

The mission to retrieve the flag and seal of Liberia from the Krahn shrine in Gedeh started when a prophetess Meemee Swen, a prominent woman of God in Liberia commonly known in the Christian circles as "Sister Wonders," approached me while I was in exile in Nigeria. She said she had an assignment concerning the spiritual cleansing of the presidential offices at the executive mansion. It was believed that due to the involvement of evil spirits and activities in the country in the past, it was necessary for an exorcism at the mansion to allow the president to officially operate free from demonic influence. According to Sister Wonders, my involvement in this operation would be very significant, given my background as a traditional priest and spiritual advisor to the former president. Hence she extended to me an invitation to Liberia from Nigeria, and I consented.

Significant among the many things that we did at this national call was the prayer to cleanse the presidential seat and other ministerial posts that were defiled when thirteen government officials were killed by a firing squad just behind the

Barclay Training Center Barracks by Master Sergeant Samuel Kanyon Doe and members of the ruling People's Redemption Council. It was revealed that the perpetration of this gruesome act attracted some curses to the presidential and other ministerial seats. I left this assignment with much displeasure, because the officials occupying those various positions, including the president, did not take the prophetic action seriously (maybe due to their spiritual immaturity).

About a year later, I was in Ghana preparing for a crusade I was to attend in southwest Cameroon, when Mama (Reverend Ezidilim Giwa-Amu), founder of New Dawn Ministries, asked that I immediately come to Lagos for some important information. To my amazement, Sister Wonders met me there with Mama Giwa-Amu. Both talked to me about another assignment in which they believed I could play a key role. Sister Wonders said the Lord had asked her to retrieve the national flag and seal that had been buried in the Krahn shrine. Sister Wonders intimated to me that I was the only person who would be able to get these national emblems because, according to her, I knew the way since I was the priest in charge when those emblems were buried. I had symbolically done this before, but Sister Wonders said that the Lord wanted us to do it physically and literally.

I canceled my crusade in Cameroon to attend to this national assignment in Liberia. Mama Giwa-Amu, knowing my irritation over the earlier assignment, thought I should make the decision without her influence. I agreed because the assignment concerned our nation. So we left Lagos for Monrovia on August 18, 2007. We had less than a week to get the flag and seal, since we were about seven days away from Flag Day (August 24). Sister Wonders said the Lord instructed her to officially present them to the presidency by August 24, with the intent of restoring the flag and seal to their original place. A team of about twenty people were put together for prayer support and the execution of this delicate assignment.

On August 19, 2007, we assembled at Kakata in Magibi County for three days of prayer and preparation. At Kakata, I was demonically struck down with paralysis because someone on the team had somehow leaked the whole plan. The entire team began to pray more vigorously and seriously because they knew the importance of my role in this all-important assignment. When I recovered, I decided that we move closer to my county so we could make a move in the night. Fear gripped most of the members on the mission as they realized the danger, but I had reached the point of no return. As the saying goes, "If it must be done, it must be done now."

At about 5:30 a.m. on August 21, 2007, we set out for Putu Jawodee, the closest town to the mountain where the shrine was located. By midnight we were at our target point. I then realized that our mission was going to be more difficult than I had thought, because we were going to use a longer route to avoid being seen by the villagers. I was not too sure of the route due to some landslides that had taken place around the mountain. We finally decided to go to the village, believing God for what to do. Initially, I thought of making an open challenge to my tribal men to show them where power lies between my God and their gods. But God has a way of fighting for Himself. He had it all planned out in His own easy and special way.

When we got to the town, the people were all shocked. Some of them were crying because they had not seen me for a long time. Others were disappointed that I had not been able to attend the funeral of the oldest man in the family who had died a few months earlier, a traditional requirement for every well-meaning member of that family. The Lord graciously opened my eyes to see the opportunity in this misfortune of the death of the old man. I asked to be taken to the graveside of the old man in order to pay him homage and show my respects. This was not just for homage per se; this was a great opportunity to get closer to the shrine where the flag and the seal had been buried. I was escorted to the traditional graveside by my cousin.

As we approached the area, my cousin had to stay behind since it was a sacred area, but because of my former office as the chief priest, I could enter into every sacred terrain. I went past the burial site and sped straight to the shrine. I then desecrated the area with kola nuts, one of the major taboos, and holy anointing oil, picked up the flag and seal and hid them under my clothes. Then I headed back my cousin, who had no idea what had transpired. I speedily met up with the rest of the team members to leave the town.

Earlier, I had introduced the other members of the party to the town as visitors coming from a nearby town. We had planned for them to wait for me at a particular junction far from the town. From the shrine, I went straight to meet them, and we took off for Kakata, where the rest of the team members were waiting for us. I knew that the shrine attendants and the elders would soon know what had been done to their shrine, and knew we should be vigilant. We were more than halfway to Kakata when one of the women in our car exclaimed, "Oh my God!" Startled, we all asked her in unison what that expression was all about. She explained, "While in the village the Lord had laid it upon my heart to rescue the three little children of Joshua's cousin who went with him to the shrine."

"Why didn't you say this when we were in the village?" I asked. At that point it was too late to go back to the town, as the alarm had probably been blown.

By the grace of God Almighty, we got to Kakata, met the rest of the team and handed over the flag and the seal to Sister Wonder and the other leaders. With tears of unspeakable joy, we all thanked God in prayers, praise, and worship for what He had done with us and through us. Only a few could really understand that this was a move toward the total freedom of the Liberian leadership, because the flag and the seal represent the sovereign identity and mandatory authority of the people respectively. The flag and seal had been buried at the shrine of the Krahns for the sole purpose of gaining perpetual control and influence over the people of Liberia. As far as the Krahn tribe was concerned, its members must be the only people to rule Liberia, with the notion that we were the ones who redeemed the country from the 133-year-rule of the Americo-Liberians.

As soon as I switched on my mobile phone, I received a phone call that shocked me to the spine. My cousin who led me to the graveside had been beheaded, along with his wife and his three children, the very children the Lord spoke about to the lady on the team. Apparently the removal of the national emblems and desecration of the shrine was discovered not long after we had left my village for Kakata. The priests and elders perceived my cousin as the immediate possible ally, since they knew that he accompanied me to the bush.

I grieved to think that if the lady had heeded the Lord's warning to take my cousin's children back with her to Monrovia, the murder may have been averted. I am certain this cousin of mine was helpless as he tried to save the children and his wife. Had their children not been around, he could have possibly escaped with his wife. I had to learn the hard way never to take lightly a word from the Lord—delays in seconds can cost a life or many.

At that point, Sister Wonder and the other leading members of the team recommended I leave quickly for Nigeria. I initially thought it was a good idea, so I immediately went packing. But then I heard the Lord tell me clearly to stay, because His assignment for me in Liberia had not ended. Sister Wonders was discontented with my decision, since she thought my presence would draw retaliation from my Krahn tribesmen.

My host at this time was William V.S. Tubman Jr., the son of the 18th president of Liberia. "Daddy Shad," as we call him, is now an evangelist seriously doing a good work for the Kingdom. Contemplating possible hideouts, I decided to visit Solili, a place notoriously identified with armed robbers, drug peddlers, and other social outcasts. Solili by definition means "Death is better than life." I decided to go there because I knew I would be much safer with them than any other group, given that those who were possibly coming after me are equally the enemies of Solili. The guys at Solili were ready at all times to contend with anyone who attempted to disturb their relative peace. According to them, they were where they were as a result of what society brought upon them, and they were ready to pay back. When I arrived at Solili, the Lord led me to share the Word with some of these young men and women, and many of them gave their lives to Christ. It was an amazing experience to see people surrendering the weapons intended for robbery and other criminal operations. In one night, more than one hundred people gave their lives to Christ amid tears and sorrow.

Around this time I had a call from Bishop John Kun Kun, my father in the Lord. He instructed me to take his place at the Flag Day ceremony, which was to occur the next morning at Bethel Cathedral in Congo Town, Monrovia. I tried hard to excuse myself from this assignment, considering the possible danger, but to no avail. Who was I to say no to my spiritual authority? Little did I know that the Lord had great plans for my life and was about to walk me into His ultimate purpose of freedom for me.

The next morning while preparing for the program, the Lord laid it upon my heart to take along some of the guys who had given their lives to Christ the night before. This was a strange move, but I obeyed. With the help of Daddy Shad, I arranged for two buses, selected about fifty of the guys, and got them all t-shirts with the inscription "God Bless Liberia" and "I am proud to be a Liberian" back and front.

## FLAG DAY CEREMONY

We got to the grounds for the celebration at about 9:00 a.m. on August 24, 2007. The place was beautifully decorated, with a detailed program line-up. There were thirteen speakers in total. I was supposed to be the eighth speaker, standing in for Bishop John Kun Kun. When I was finally introduced, everybody was astonished. Nobody expected me there. Many of those present had only heard of me, but had not seen me after my conversion to the Christian faith.

My presentation was on the significance of the flag. I went on to talk about how we risked our lives to recover the original flag and seal. I also went on to talk about how the Church was failing to reach out to the outcasts of the Liberian society. I challenged the gathering that it was the responsibility of the Church to restore Liberia to God's ultimate place of purpose. At this point, I asked the men from Solili to rise up and be seen, and they rose up. Everybody at the meeting that day cried, including many top dignitaries from the presidency and members of the diplomatic corps. People immediately started making pledges of contribution to help get those young guys off the streets and back into society. This ignited the rehabilitation program in Liberia to reshape the lives of the ex-child soldiers.

In the evening, I heard the Truth and Reconciliation Commission (TRC) making its appeal for perpetrators as well as victims and witnesses to come and present their preliminary statements to the committee. I decided to answer their appeal.

## TRUTH VERSUS JUSTICE

I remember the day I walked into the TRC building on 9th Street. I was stopped at the reception area because the secretary said I was not appropriately dressed. I was wearing shorts and a t-shirt with a pair of sneakers. I asked why they had a dress code for ex-soldiers and victims. They did not know who was speaking to them at this time. When I introduced myself to them, they all ran for cover!

I asked to speak to the director of the commission and I insisted I make my statement that day. They took my preliminary statement, after which I also appealed to the commission to be one of the first perpetrators to appear for the opening hearings before the commission. Many people advised me to change my mind, but I told them there was no way I could deny it, because it was and is the truth. Normally, anytime I speak the truth I feel free and relieved.

I knew the implication of showing up at the TRC. I was going to be tried, and if found guilty, which was likely, I would be recommended for prosecution, which meant I could be either jailed for life or killed. However, I did not relent. I spoke the truth. For a season, it came to the point where I had only two days free in a whole week, because I was in the safe house under the TRC supervision for the other days. I used those two days to make restitution by preaching to people and asking for forgiveness.

I sometimes went to notorious areas where ex-combatants rejected by their families and society were hiding and doing all kinds of evil to the community. I knew my days with them were limited, so I wanted to do something among them to help take the pain away. These guys were living and hiding in graveyards, and would go from there to commit crimes. There was no police to arrest them or put them in check.

Knowing that the country had just come out of war obviously became a big deterrent to investors, so a lot of people realized it was prudent to support me in this endeavor. The government was also happy with what I was doing, although they did not come out openly to support the work. However, many people feared that it was risky for a former general to work together with ex-combatants. They thought I could instigate an uprising.

After all the results were compiled by TRC, Liberia's President Ellen Johnson Sirleaf got the hint that my name was first on the list for prosecution. Fearing that I would get into a lot of trouble if I continued seeing the TRC, she tried to persuade me to leave town. It was part of this persuasive move by the president that led me to meet Bishop Duncan Williams of the Christian Action Faith Ministries in Ghana. He also advised me out of love to keep myself from the TRC and have a fresh start in life somewhere else in the world.

I understood why they were all giving me this advice. However, I stood my ground and insisted on facing the truth, even when justice did not seem like it was going to favor me. Even though I knew it could lead to my death, I wanted to face the truth for two reasons. First, I did not want to walk anywhere looking over my shoulders, afraid of who was coming after me. Second, I knew I owed it to the people of Liberia and posterity to tell them what really happened. I never thought I was physically going to come out free and not be jailed, yet at the same time I was free in my mind and that was good enough.

Another crucial matter that made me face the TRC was this: I had many people who forgave me, even though they had not heard the full truth. Thus, I wanted to be elaborate in my explanation so that those people could understand the whole truth and reconsider whether or not they could still forgive me. I believed this would usher in the genuine forgiveness that I was yearning for.

I met the TRC after my preliminary statements. And as I said earlier, I was the first on the list of those recommended for prosecution. Many people said I was only claiming and faking Christianity to avoid punishment from the hands of justice, but my appearance at the TRC was enough evidence that I really had nothing to hide. If I was sentenced to death, it would still have added to my testimony that for the sake of Christ I was not afraid to die by telling the truth. If I was sentenced to life imprisonment, it was still a privilege to share Christ with others I would meet in prison. Should I be set free, the four corners of the earth would become my evangelistic field. So, it really was not me, but the devil that was in a quandary concerning my case.

Interestingly, on the day of my hearing, no one came out to make a case against me. Among the many former generals and all other perpetrators of many atrocities committed during the war, I became the first person recommended to be given a resounding and unconditional amnesty. All charges against me were dropped. It appeared as if nothing had ever happened at all—a confirmation of the clean slate the Lord had given me when He arrested and forgave me long before the TRC summoned me. The TRC's amnesty was just a physical manifestation of the spiritual work that Jesus Christ had done in my life. Truly, he who the Lord sets free is free indeed!

In order to ruin this freedom I have in Christ Jesus, the devil has furiously attacked me on numerous occasions. I miraculously survived a car accident where I had to endure a broken rib and bruises in many other areas of my body. I have come through several assassination attempts where armed men sought me both in homes and the streets. I have also had to tolerate several physical assaults and many insults. Disappointingly for the enemy, none of these batterings has been able to rob me of the great freedom the Almighty has lavished upon me through Jesus Christ, my Savior and Lord. Free at last! Free at last! Thank God, I'm free at last—and nothing else compares!

However, we are not ignorant to the devices of the enemy. He fights today, retreats and fights again and again. Ever since I received Christ, the devil has been fighting me. The fight continues unabated. Having survived all of Satan's attacks thus far, I humbly solicit the prayers of my Christian brothers and sisters. Let not the devil destroy this wonderful testimony, by which people of contrary beliefs may be converted.

# THE SINNER'S PRAYER

*I have sinned against You, O Lord. Forgive me. Accept me into Your plan for humankind once again. I thought I had lost all meaning for living and could no longer be restored. But if You can save Brother Joshua, you can also save me from... (pronounce whatever you know as a stronghold on you).*

Believe God has forgiven you and thank Him for it. Then ask God to lead you to a church or pastor where you can be taught His ways. As God blessed me, so are you blessed—and even more blessings are coming your way as you remain steadfast.

# ABOUT THE AUTHOR

Headlined as "the most evil men in the world" in a major United Kingdom online news publication, Joshua Milton Blahyi has been interviewed by media worldwide. His life as a violent warlord began at age 11 when he carried out his first human sacrifice—and takes responsibility for 20,000 deaths during the time he was controlled by Satan during Liberia's civil war years.

He has been preaching God's Good News for more than a decade and is married with four children. Pastor Blahyi and his family live in Liberia.

## A WORD FROM THE AUTHOR'S WIFE, JOSIE BLAHYI

Evangelist Joshua Milton Blahyi is my husband, and he is a very nice, jovial, and down-to-earth person. He has been serving the Lord for fourteen years now. He is a man of integrity, and is also a carrier of God's power, presence, and anointing. Joshua is very lively and cheerful as he fathers our four children. I do not see him as other people may see him. I am convinced in my heart of hearts that he is a new person indeed. There is no trace of his past. I miss him every second whenever he is away from home on missions, but the Lord told me what I was getting into when He revealed to me Joshua, my hero, as my husband.

# IN THE RIGHT HANDS, THIS BOOK WILL CHANGE LIVES!

Most of the people who need this message will not be looking for this book. To change their lives, you need to put a copy of this book in their hands.

> *But others (seeds) fell into good ground, and brought forth fruit, some a hundred-fold, some sixty-fold, some thirty-fold* (Matthew 13:8).

Our ministry is constantly seeking methods to find the good ground, the people who need this anointed message to change their lives. Will you help us reach these people?

> *Remember this—a farmer who plants only a few seeds will get a small crop. But the one who plants generously will get a generous crop* (2 Corinthians 9:6).

## EXTEND THIS MINISTRY BY SOWING
### 3 BOOKS, 5 BOOKS, 10 BOOKS, OR MORE TODAY,
#### AND BECOME A LIFE CHANGER!

Thank you,

Don Nori Sr., Founder
Destiny Image
Since 1982